"When my wife, Barbara, and I were approached to write this endorsement, I felt greatly honored, as I truly believe Patrick's story will inspire and bring hope to those struggling with addiction and a desire to be free from homosexuality. As a senior Pastor of Victory Outreach Albuquerque for over 33 years, I have seen countless miracles, transformations, recovery, and I've heard so many inspiring stories from all over the world. Patrick's transformation was something so special and I knew there was a special anointing on him from the start.

We met Patrick, a then addict, as he entered our ministries' men's recovery center called Victory Home in Albuquerque, NM in 2016. During his stay in our recovery home, he disclosed that he had also been involved in homosexuality, which is something he passionately desired to be set free from. We remember a conversation when he said that he believed God called him to help bring people out of the lifestyle.

After seeing his journey and the amazing transformation that has taken place in his life, we believe that it is time that he shares his story with the world. His testimony in his book, *'Open My Encrypted Heart'* can help so many people. Scripture tells us: "He who the Son sets free, is free indeed." We truly believe in Patrick's story – we believe you will be inspired and blessed. It is a prime example of just how powerful the Gospel of Jesus Christ is!"

Pastor Danny & Barbara Sanchez
Victory Outreach International Ministries

"Patrick Quezada fervently recounts his personal journey, delving into past missteps and obstacles, life devoid of God, and the profound metamorphosis that arose from embracing God's unconditional love, pursuing His presence, and uncovering his identity in Him."

J Brett Salazar
Entrepreneur, Influencer, Founder of J Brett's Journey

"There is nothing more precious than intimacy with God. He meets us where we are and draws us with relationship—not mere religion. I witnessed some of Patrick's best times as well as his worst. He is uncompromisingly honest. He's never failed to return to intimacy with God—no matter how many times he ran away because of past hurts. Patrick is an example of resilience and perseverance. God wants him to share all He's done for him. I am grateful to have overcome the enemy by God's grace. I've been blessed by Patrick's testimony and creativity. I believe you will find hope and inspiration within.

Victor Franco
Artist & Writer of plays and fiction/non-fiction works

"Over my many years as a church Pastor, I have witnessed addiction destroy many loving people. *'Open My Encrypted Heart'* is one man's journey to find healing from the pain of addiction while holding on to God's purposes for his life. Through his own discovery of the original meaning of the rainbow and of God's subsequent promises to us all - Patrick Quezada's story is a much needed encouragement for a community that has often been neglected and rejected by religion. Patrick's heart for the LGBTQIA+ is genuine, and emulates the kind of love that Jesus gave and commanded us all to give. This book will inspire diverse and desolate souls longing to find true love and real freedom!"

Troy Lewis
Lead Pastor, Steamboat Christian Center in Steamboat Springs, Co

---

"Between the covers of *'Open My Encrypted Heart'* readers discover treasures and riches from the soul of author Patrick Quezada. His spiritual life – along with untold thousands of precious women and men – is inspired by Isaiah 45: 2-3. In these biblical verses, God promises treasures of darkness and hidden riches of secret places. The words are sacred promises to Patrick, and to the ministry Victory Outreach. Like its founder Pastor Sonny Arguinzoni Sr, Patrick's chains to drug and alcohol bondages broke through the power of God. As men laid hands on and prayed in Holy Spirit power for him, Patrick surrendered homosexuality to the Lordship of Jesus Christ. The Savior's love for Patrick unlocked his soul to true treasures and riches – a relationship with Christ Jesus, who heals broken hearts. If you're looking for spiritual wealth, then you'll find rich deposits of gold and silver on these pages."

Steve Rees
Journalist/News Writer

"I have known Patrick Quezada for nearly 4 years through the Freedom March group and events. I can say that he is truly a man that is sincere and transparent in the journey of freedom and healing in knowing him. His book, *'Open My Encrypted Heart'* talks about the journey with all that he has dealt with in terms of rejection, addiction, homosexuality and other forms of brokenness. He tells his story to see others get healed and set free in the same way that God has been doing in his life. Many of us have walked along with Patrick in this journey to seeing God's redemptive and restoring work in his life in which I hope his book of his testimony will be a true blessing to you as well as you read it."

Jon Sowell
Rainbow Revival/Freedom March/Lover of the Gospel

"Patrick's story of transformation illustrates the hope we can only find in Jesus. His poetry is raw and real, giving hope to those who are trying to discover what it means to be a man of God. In an age where people are struggling to find their true identity, especially in regards to sexuality, Patrick's journey provides insight on the battle within."

Chaille Brindley
Author of Organic Faith and Christian blogger

"I have known Patrick for several years and witnessed him rising out the ashes of what would appear to be utter destruction. Through an Encrypted Heart, you will discover how Patrick is resilient as well as victorious over obstacles, shame and addiction time after time. Proverbs 24:16 tells us that a righteous man falls seven times but rises again. We know it's not our righteousness as ours is of filthy rags. This freedom and sobriety is not possible solely on our own strength but as we surrender to the strength of the Lord Jesus and live according to the spirit instead of the destructive desires of our flesh.

Revelation 12:11 communicates that we will be overcome by the blood of the Lamb and the word of our testimony. As you read, *'Open My Encrypted Heart'* and Patrick's testimony in comparison to former expressions and art expressions that Patrick is a constant overcomer! Philippians 1:6 "being confident of this very thing, that He who has begun a good work in you will complete it until the day of Jesus Christ." The Lord is constantly working on, in and through us. We are seeing the Lord take the old mess and mold him into a masterpiece."

Pastor Chris Roche
Ignite Church International in Brighton, Colorado

"This young budding poet and my dear friend Patrick; shows great promise with his debut work! Although a longtime writer, as far as I can remember. His writing is infused with a fresh voice, raw emotion, and a willingness to explore the depths of human experience. With each line, he demonstrates a keen sense of observation, a talent for language, and a passion for telling his story. Such a remarkable ability to evoke feelings and spark connections with his readers. I eagerly anticipate seeing my friend's growth and evolution as a poet, and I have no doubt that his pages, his lines, his words will resonate with many."

Michael Sanchez
Longtime Friend, Influencer

OPEN MY ENCRYPTED HEART

Copyright 2024, Patrick Quezada.
All rights reserved.

No portion of this book may be reproduced by mechanical, photographic, or electronic process; nor may it be stored in a retrieval system, transmitted in any form, or otherwise be copied for public use or private use without written permission of the copyright owner.

It is sold with the understanding that the publisher and the individual author are not engaged in the rendering of psychological, legal, accounting, or other professional advice.

The content and views in this book are the sole expression and opinion of the author and not necessarily the views of Fig Factor Media, LLC.

For More Information:

Fig Factor Media | figfactormedia.com
Patrick Quezada | openmyencryptedheart.com

Cover Design by LDG Marco Alvarez
Cover Layout by LDG Juan Manuel Serna Rosales

Printed in the United States of America

ISBN: 978-1-961600-02-7
Library of Congress Number: 2024909493

Rated M for mature. This book is written for mature audiences. Throughout the book, there are strong themes of explicit language, alcohol and drug use, homosexuality, violence, death, and sexual assault.

Patrick Quezada

OPEN

MY ENCRYPTED HEART

DEDICATION

Throughout this journey, you will read many poems, church sermons and notes, journal entries, encouraging personal Facebook Posts, song lyrics that I've written, and other pieces that highlight monumental milestones in my life. I hope and pray that you enjoy this book dedicated to my Heavenly Father, my Lord and Savior Jesus Christ, my beautiful mommy Rosemarie Quezada, and in loving memory of my beloved best friend David Helding as much as I do! This book was co-written with the Holy Spirit.

Godspeed, PQ

TABLE OF CONTENTS

Acknowledgments 10
Foreword by Rosemarie Quezada.. 11
Preface - My Testimony 14
Rainbow Revival... 26

Part 1: From Heartbeat to Heartbreak 29
Part 2: The Bound and Broken Heart 79
Part 3: Haunted. Hunted. Healed 161
Part 4: Pulling On Heartstrings & Other Things 215
Part 5: Final Reflections for The Soul 273

Special Artwork..285
About the Author...288

ACKNOWLEDGMENTS

This book's idea and concept has been a God-given, inspirational assignment since 2008. My poem portfolio has grown to nearly 300 poems to date. Narrowing it down to one story has been difficult.

I am eternally grateful for this beautiful dream to become a reality thanks to my Heavenly Father's Amazing Grace, my mother Rosemarie Quezada for her continued love and encouragement, my other mother Helen Gomez, my Freedom March/Rainbow Revival Family, my Victory Outreach Family, Jacqueline Ruiz, Gaby Hernandez and the rest of the Fig Factor Media Publishing team!

FOREWORD

To My Dear Son Patrick,

As I sit down to write these words, my heart increases with pride and overwhelming gratitude for the journey we have walked through together. It has been a path sown with obstacles, pain, and tears, but through it all, we have emerged stronger, wiser, and more closely knit together by God's grace, and guidance more than ever before.

When you first stumbled into the gripping backpack of addiction, little did you know the Holy Spirit had already uncovered the world we would both face shattered into a million shards of fear, worry, and helplessness. I watched as the bright light of your heart, and soul dimmed beneath the suffocating weight of substance abuse. My days and nights blurred into an endless cycle of disappointment, waiting, whispered prayers to our Heavenly Father, and endless nights of intercession for your safety, your surrender, and most importantly your soul!

As a mother, for a season I battled with my own feelings of guilt, self-doubt, and despair. I questioned where I had gone wrong, what signs had I missed, and how I could have possibly failed to protect you from the clutches of the enemy? It was until I fully surrendered you to God, I finally rested in peace knowing He is in control, not me. Yet in the depths of my grieving, an ounce of determination, and faith took root within me—a merciless maternal instinct that refused to surrender you to the darkness without a fight.

Our journey through your crystal meth, and alcohol addiction was a rollercoaster of emotions—a relentless balance of highs and lows, relapses and recoveries, setbacks and small victories. But through it all, one thing remained unwavering: my unconditional love for you, my child. It was this love that carried me through the darkest nights, fueled my determination to never give up on you, and sustained me as we navigated the treacherous waters of recovery together.

I watched you stumble and fall, time and time again, but each time you rose, battered but unbroken, I saw a glimmer of hope reignite within your eyes as you continued to trust God. It was this spark of resilience, and purpose in this unwavering spirit of yours, that inspired me to stand by your side through every step of your journey towards sobriety, and restoration.

Today, as I look back on those tumultuous days of struggle and strife, I am filled with immense Godly confidence, and awe at the man of God you have become. You have weathered the storm of addiction with courage and grace, emerging on the other side as a beacon of light, strength, and inspiration to all those around you.

In sharing our story within these pages, my hope is to offer consolation, wisdom, and guidance to those who find themselves standing at the crossroads of despair and hope. As a therapist I wondered how is it so significant, with ease for me to help others, yet near impossible to reach my own son. May our journey, and words serve as a reminder that no battle is unstoppable, no darkness unending, and no love unconditional without the power of God's love, and strength. To those who have nearly lost their faith, hope, and ability to stand with their loved ones through addiction, brokenness, and unending pain. Keep standing, and never give up!

"Therefore, put on the full armor of God, so that when the day of evil comes, you may be able to stand your ground, and after you have done everything, to stand. Stand firm..." Ephesians 6:13-14 (NIV)

With all my love and unwavering support…
No more off to the races!

Your blessed mommy forever,
Rosemarie Quezada

PREFACE

My Testimony

My name is Patrick Quezada. I am a 43-year-old grateful man born in Denver, Colorado to mother Rosemarie Quezada and father Frank Wanczyk. I have always had a very close and adjoining relationship with my mom. She is not only the greatest mother I could have asked for, she is also my best friend, and greatest support and discipline. As an ordained Pastor and a licensed Christian therapist, my mother has been the biggest spiritual example of how to trust in God and how to follow Him, especially through the trials brought on by a broken life. At times, she has also been my biggest trigger, extremely critical with "tough love." Sadly, I have disappointed her many times by not meeting her high standards. I am so proud of her accomplishments, though, and extremely grateful to have her in my life. If it weren't for her prayers, I don't think I would be where I am today. She is a real life Wonder Woman and my God-sent back bone when I wasn't able to stand on my own.

My father, on the other hand, was hardly there for me the way a son needs a loving dad and male role model. Over the years, I would see him time to time, but we never truly bonded or shared a genuine love and fellowship. Unfortunately, addiction has played a huge part in my family for generations. My dad loved his pedestal-placed wife and her family deemed more than me, his own son.

Growing up, it was normal to see my family buying cases of beer, cracking open bottles of booze, popping pills, and smoking weed for any occasion including birthday parties, Fourth of July, and Christmas. When I was in school, I experienced my first encounter of a loved one dying of addiction. My uncle Mark died of cirrhosis at the young age of 27. It was heartbreaking.

Being without a dad for many years wasn't a loss in my eyes. It gave me the loving privilege to grow up with not one, but two loving mothers. Helen was more than I could ask for. I will forever cherish the memories of decorating during the holidays. Just mom, Helen, and me.

Many of my cousins and aunts were gay or bisexual. This was normal for us. I attended my first gay pride festival before the age of ten. Growing up, I played with Barbie dolls, wanted to be Wonder Woman, and started to look at boys with curiosity. This is who I became.

I grew up Catholic until I was about 15. But I have always had a lot of love and respect for God, even if I didn't have a personal relationship with Him. One day, mom was invited to a Christian church. She received a personal encounter with God. That was enough for her to fully surrender her life to Jesus. A year later, my friend in high school outed me to my mother because of an argument we had. Mom became depressed and isolated herself. I was devastated and afraid to go home. Mom's worst fear came true; her son was now gay. She went through a roller coaster of emotions. I told her there was nothing she or God could do to change my mind. I am gay, and I will live my life this way.

With our spirits and our lifestyles now conflicting, I went off the deep end. I started making friends with people who also felt like misfits; rejects who bonded through vanity, sex, drugs, and a lot of parties. I had always been a straight "A" student involved in everything from ROTC, drama, speech, choir, and the swim team. Junior year, I ended a relationship with the only girlfriend I ever had shortly after the junior prom. Senior year, I did something that had never been done at my conservative high school: I took my boyfriend to the senior prom. Very nervous of how others would treat us, I went all in. As we slow danced together, we received a standing ovation.

Soon college came. I attended only one semester before dropping out. During this time, I rebelled against God, and started exploring with Ouija boards and horoscopes. This was the beginning of many years of being an alcoholic and a serial monogamist looking for love in all the wrong places. Always a people pleaser who put others before myself, I jumped from relationship to relationship wanting to feel loved and accepted.

In September 2011, I found out my partner of five years had given me HIV. I was devastated. How could this have happen? I coped by drinking and crying over Alanis Morissette records. I felt ashamed, used, and lost. Wreaking havoc in every way imaginable, I was now like the walking dead. What started as drinking a bottle of vodka a day, soon turned to ecstasy, and a very dark world of crystal meth. "PNP" party and play sex addiction was my new outlet. Every night, I would get online using Grindr, Adam4Adam, and every other hook up app to seek my next encounter. During this time, I was also very involved in amateur porn.

As an empty shell of my former self, all I knew was how to blow clouds and have sexual encounters with a lot of men. Soon it became a game to me to see how many men I could get, including straight men who may have been married. Public sex was another thrill I once sought. When I took a needle to my arm, I lost all sense of dignity and fell deeper into shame. One thing that I was always careful of, thank God, was disclosing my HIV status.

One night while cruising online, I ran into a friend who invited me to his sex party with lots of men, porn, and dope. He told me that a friend of his would soon pick me up to head over. As the truck pulled up, it was then I met a man who would later become my ex. I couldn't tell you who else was at the party that night. All I know is there was something very attractive about him. We exchanged numbers and became inseparable.

Over the next two years, our relationship became very toxic. We were physically and emotionally co-dependent and violent toward each other as we fell deeper into crystal. He pulled me along for quite a ride into the dope scene that I wish I had never taken part in. The worst moment with him started with a shot of meth that led to being tied up and raped by him and his gang. The night of horror was recorded and sent to my mom's phone. I eventually got a restraining order against him and thought I finally got rid of this monster. I soon met a lot of very intense addicts, dealers, and criminals.

Tired of being homeless, and wasting away at 140 pounds, I fell into paranoia, anorexia, bulimia, and depression. I was on Lithium, benzos, and many other psych meds. I was on a fast track toward the devil. Running from my violent and very obsessed ex, the monster was back and I was slowly killing myself. I was now shooting up at least two times a day, and I had nowhere to go except back to my mom's house. The worst thing I ever put mom through was her getting arrested for my bad choices. My ex had a storage unit that was raided by the police. In this unit were engraving plates to make fake hundred dollar bills, printing paper to make fake social security cards, birth certificates, blank payroll checks, stolen IDs, and many passports with his photo and different names on it. He put me down as an emergency contact for the storage unit without me knowing. I tried to remove myself from this crazy situation and wanted nothing to do with it. One of our actions was to get a restraining order against him, and he was not happy about it. He proceeded to get one against us by lying and saying that we were harassing him. The judge believed him, and my mom and I were thrown in jail.

After he finally left me alone, I met a man who became my rebound. Gay marriage became legal in Colorado. We wasted no time and got married. Our life together seemed normal. We didn't use drugs and hardly drank alcohol. We were homebodies who worked normal jobs. Finally, it seemed my fairytale relationship had come true. We were happily married with our own place and our dog named Khloe. One day his ex emailed me and said, "Patrick, you need to know who you're married to. Google his name!" So, I did. I found out that he was a convicted sex offender. Crushed again, I filed for a divorce, went back to meth, and ran off to the races once again. Realizing I no longer wanted to run, I asked mom for help. She introduced me to Victory Outreach in 2016.

I made a decision to leave Colorado. My aunt bought me a bus ticket to Albuquerque, New Mexico. When I went into the recovery home, I was finally open for a change. I was so broken, and hit rock bottom so many times, I knew I was going to die and needed a miracle. I surrendered my life to Jesus Christ. He began the process of setting me free from meth, alcohol, meds, depression, bitterness, and witchcraft. During my stay at Victory Outreach, I was actively involved in ministry. It felt amazing to finally surrender my hurting heart.

The Outreach is a faith-based Recovery Home that focuses on rescuing Treasures Out Of Darkness who have been beaten up by the streets in the inner cities; mainly drug addicts, alcoholics, gang members, and prostitutes. Victory Outreach not only focuses on deliverance from substance abuse, but also helps hurting souls find dignity, a relationship with God, and a purpose-driven life! I served in the ministry for three years. I had meaning in my life. Learning to pray, read the Bible, and fast was a blessing.

Going into the home, I surrendered fully from addiction. Two days later, I experienced complete deliverance. Facing zero withdrawal symptoms led me to make a promise to God that no matter how hard things get, I will trust and follow Him. I also started to love myself. This led me to the desire of turning away from homosexuality and relationships to fully focus on the relationship with myself and most of all a relationship with my Higher Power Jesus Christ. I came to the realization that I cannot control my unmanageable life by myself. I needed help. Jesus Christ helped me forgive myself.

There were many troubles I had to work out in recovery. One of which concerned my best friend David. We were like brothers, always in the bars together. One Sunday, we decided to go to Happy Hour. We had unlimited beer in our bellies. But still, David wanted more. I was pretty drunk and was done for the night. So, I decided to get high on meth with my ex instead. David went to another bar alone. The next morning, I received a phone call from a friend saying that David crashed into a lake and drowned. Drunk driving killed my best friend. I felt responsible because I wasn't there and couldn't save him. I carried this guilt and anger for years.

God softened my heart in the recovery home to forgive myself. Nothing I did, or didn't do, could save my friend from addiction, because I couldn't save myself. In fact, if I had gone with him to the second bar, I could have also lost my life too.

After graduating from the recovery home, I was freer than ever. God blessed me with not only one, but two jobs: Amazon and Door Dash. I got my license back after not having it for 13 years because of two DUIs. I was also blessed with a car. I never thought anyone or anything could restore my life.

I had now been clean for three and a half years. In 2020, I left Victory Outreach and went to another church. I met a Pastor who wanted to disciple me. He offered to get an apartment with me and be my accountability/sober support partner. Everything was great in the beginning. But six months later, I noticed inappropriate behaviors and conversations. On my birthday, he gave me a dozen red roses and many gifts. Feeling uncomfortable, I went to dinner with my friends and made the mistake of drinking that night. When my friends dropped me off at home, I blacked out. The next morning I woke up to find out my roommate, the Pastor, and supposed man of God, had sexually assaulted me. I was completely naked and so disgusted, and angry at God for allowing this to happen.

I ran from God and the church. I did the only thing I knew. I got high. I relapsed hard for seven months. Destroying my life, the best I could, I no longer had hope. One day, I met a guy to get high with, and took a shot that nearly took my life. It not only had meth, it was also cut with Fentynol and GHB (the date rape drug).

After coming down, I had fully detached the retina in my right eye and lost most of my vision. God spoke clearly to me in that moment saying, "If your eye causes you to sin, pluck it out!" He also said that He loved me so much, and was sorry for what happened to me. He assured me that He was still with me, and wanted me to run back into His arms. It was then I realized it's not His fault. There are good and bad people in the church as well as good and bad in the world.

I reached out to my good friend at the time, Tyler, a director of the LIT Movement Sober Living in Cincinnati. He asked if I was tired of running and if I wanted God to heal my brokenness? I surrendered again and flew to Ohio. I checked into Woodhaven, a rehab center, and made amends with myself and with God. My eye never recovered, sadly it grew worse. I was taken to the ER where I was told I needed surgery. During my time in the hospital, I caught COVID-19 and became very sick. As I had to quarantine, I found myself in the lion's den at Gateway Men's Shelter where drugs were everywhere. I stayed strong, and refused to use. Passing this test was a huge victory.

I came back to Woodhaven and finally finished something. I graduated from the program with destiny, hope, and dignity. To God be all the glory! Because of my obedience to stay faithful, God blessed me with a beautiful family at the LIT Movement. The day after I graduated, we went white water rafting in West Virginia. Since then, I went on to work for a program called Short Term Refuge (STR). Taking addicts, and alcoholics off of the street and housing them for seven days for their recovery. I was once homeless and hopeless, so I could empathize. I received my peer recovery support specialist certification, was a leader of Celebrate Recovery, on the worship team, and had completed nearly 18 months of recovery. Since then, I have faced various trials, including a huge fallout with Tyler and Cincinnati, and battled an ongoing rejection spirit leading to repetitive cycles of bad behavior.

Still learning how to trust, I now have the tools and the knowledge to move forward with God's help guiding me every step of the way. I find every possible way to spread hope through loving and encouraging others! I actively go to meetings, work the Twelve Steps daily, attend church regularly, and work for the United States Postal Service in Steamboat Springs, Colorado.

I once had the opportunity and privilege to be a frontline hero. To give back to the world after being the one taking from others was such a blessing. I would also like to testify that I am now undetectable and HIV-free! My God is a healer and a miracle worker. God also started the process to heal the relationship with my father.

I am not perfect. I have made a lot of mistakes including falling back into the gay lifestyle after seven years of abstinence and nearly getting married again, but I thank God, my convictions pulled me from making that decision. I'm not where I'd like to be, but I am not where I once was! If He can love me enough to rescue me, anyone can have hope! All it takes is a willing and surrendered heart.

God has reignited the fire in my spirit, and I am grateful for the gifts and creativity He has given me. Over the years I have written hundreds of poems.

This book, 'Open My Encrypted Heart' has been quite a journey in the making! As far as relationships go, I have continued to stay true to my promise to God, and will continue to stay single and practice celibacy. I have been single for many years, and no longer am defined by any labels of sexuality or drug addiction. I describe my identity as a "Man of God" who deserves love, hope, and forgiveness. Thank You Heavenly Father for another chance to live for You, and not my broken past! Always looking for love in all the wrong places, my once encrypted heart has finally been opened by the one relationship that I have always longed for, the one with God.

Words of worship (from the bible, sermons from Pastors and mentors, and of my own writing) saved me. They helped me see the light of God and led me to my path. I hope this book can do the same for you.

Patrick Quezada
from DRAG...to DRUGS to DELIVERED!

RAINBOW REVIVAL

rain·bow

N**oun:** An arch of colors formed in the sky in certain circumstances, caused by the refraction and dispersion of the sun's light by rain or other water droplets in the atmosphere.

"all the colors of the rainbow"
any display of the colors of the spectrum produced by dispersion of light.
a wide range or variety of related and typically colorful things.
"a rainbow of medals decorated his chest"

The rainbow has ALWAYS been an important element in my life. When I was actively in the LGBTQ community, it was a symbol of pride and unity to walk with others who were rejected or thrown away because of same sex attraction.

As a believer and a follower of Jesus, the rainbow represents God's promise to never flood the earth again.

And God said, "This is the sign of the covenant I am making between me and you and every living creature with you, a covenant for all generations to come:

I have set my rainbow in the clouds, and it will be the sign of the covenant between me and the earth.

Whenever I bring clouds over the earth and the rainbow appears in the clouds,

I will remember my covenant between me and you and all living creatures of every kind. Never again will the waters become a flood to destroy all life.

Whenever the rainbow appears in the clouds, I will see it and remember the everlasting covenant between God and all living creatures of every kind on the earth." Genesis 9:12-16

The enemy is trying to deceive the world and steal God's rainbow giving it false meaning.

1. **Giving it to the LGBTQ people for pride is allowing them to believe that it is a symbol for unity in their community.** If a Christian happens to mention anything about the rainbow not belonging to them, they get offended, understandingly so. Though it is true, it belongs to God, they take offense because they have been judged, and hurt by so many religious people who proclaim to be Christians but really don't know Jesus.

They have been rejected by the world; most of the community has experienced severe trauma just like I have.

I have left the LGBTQ lifestyle and have disregarded all "labels" of sexuality that the enemy has used to corrupt and cause division between the gay community and the church. The devil and his schemes need to finally be exposed bringing unity, and healing once and for all! The only label I proudly carry is a "Man of God!"

2. **The rainbow has also been a symbol in the world to represent luck and superstition.** Finding a pot of gold at the end of a rainbow is nothing more than a fairytale. This has been taught to children at a very young age, as it's even printed on a cereal box of Lucky Charms. This is witchcraft and superstition. It is not what the rainbow represents.

Leaving the world to follow Jesus, my main mission is to declare truth of healing and deliverance. Stand and reach out to those who need love and sanctification through Jesus. The enemy tried to steal the rainbow that has never been his to begin with. Taking back the rainbow is my purpose in life, and taking back God's promises from the enemy who tried to steal them!

The rainbow belongs to God, and will always belong to God!

These are the end times, and I choose to help spread truth, love, and grace to help others realize that God is the answer to all forms of identity.

God loves all people, and we all bleed the same.

PART I:
FROM HEARTBEAT TO HEARTACHE

'As in water face reflects face, so, the heart of man reflects the man.'
PROVERBS 27:19

Haze...

[#Poem #EndTimes #Revelation #Prophesy #Dreams #Vision #Discernment #WordFromGod #HolySpirit #Rapture #DrugUse #Addiction #Rated M]

Slowly fading into nothing...
This once chosen hero feels the emptiness of God's heart...
Never truly knowing his task,
the world has shaped him into a zero,
and shamed him for the last time...
No clone, or new body can make me feel worth...
Desensitized by politics, and chemical infusion...
Radiation melts my insides,
and squeezes every ounce of hope left...
Do I want to keep living?
Thrive, or barely survive?
I know many secrets spoken by God...
A prophet you could say...
God help me be more courageous
than I feel today...
No garbage trucks or cloudy smoke
will provoke fear within to lose...
Genotype, crack it back, what now do I lack?
What year is it now? Back to the future we go...
I know many things...
Will this man gain riches and angel wings?
Time will tell...
Light it up or rest well...
Here we go into a dream...
Prepare for unveiling of many things...

Love

[#Poem #Love #Fulfillment #NewLife #Forgiveness #Relationship #Romance #Companionship]

Love is what you see
Love is what you feel
Love is inside you
Inside you is love
Caring and happiness
are what love brings
So if you're feeling lonely
and sad inside
Find someone to turn to
when you feel bad inside

Open Heart (Gratitude Within)

[#Poem #Deliverance #Rededication #Surrender #Christianity #SexualSin #Addiction #Recovery #Suicide #Death #Promiscuity #MentalHealth #Faith Rated M]

As I open up my heart
this I promise You
That I will never leave You
no matter what I go through

Drugs never loved me
Lust is just a game
Taking me straight to hell
If I'd remain the same

How good the flesh will feel
As pride and ego lie
Planting suicidal thoughts
The enemy tried to get me to die

Then I fell to my knees
No longer want to be a whore
God help me please
Win this psychopathic war

Like a rushing wind
Your love has set me free
From the junkie and the pig
that I used to be
How can I be forgiven
for the chaos I have caused?

When people give me credit
I say please hold the applause
The glory goes to Him
The only One I'd give my sin
To cleanse my brokenness
Now I feel gratitude within
this brand new skin

My life I owe to You
Was blind but now I see
The wounded soul
You used to know
Is no longer defined as me

So when you hear my name
Trust I'm not the same
Guilty shameful man
Instead I choose
to follow my Father's plan

His grace is sufficient
His mercy has given me
Another chance to prove
How beautiful life can be

Prayer for Forgiveness

[#Poem #Prayer #Heartache #Relapse #Backslide #Survival #Apology #Gratitude #Obedience #Christianity]

How can I start again such a battle that I'm in?
No one can understand the pain that I feel within
To go back to my own vomit, and feel so much shame
To ignore the hand of God, I now realize
this is not a game
I was out there lost and broken barely living day by day
Yet, all God wanted me to do
was to get on my knees and pray
I am sorry, dear Lord for the pain I have caused You
Will you please forgive me?
I'm so lost without You
Will I make it into heaven or will I split hell wide-open?
God has given us free will to make our own choice
So search deep within and listen for His voice
Thank you dear Lord for making my heart anew
I promise to do my best to stay faithful
and obey everything You ask me to do

Amen.

A Shadow of My Former Self

[#Poem #Prayer #Heartache #Relapse #Backslide #Hope #Surrender #Recovery Rated M]

As I wake up in the morning, it is another day I dread
I take a look in the mirror and ponder
Where has my life been led?
Every wrinkle on my face every teardrop in my eye
To walk on broken glass, I can only wonder why?
Wanting to pick up the pieces
that I have swept under my bed
For the life that I once had
is just an illusion in my head
The path that I have chosen seems so dark and cold
Not knowing how to fly again a failure I've been told
I once was known as innocent and driven for success
I pray to God to ease my mind and put my soul to rest

Reflection (I Honor You)

[#Poem #Gratitude #Thanksgiving #Tribute #Honor #Sacrifice #Relentless #Encouragement #Christianity]

As we reflect on the things we are thankful for today

I'd like to pay tribute to the many beautiful relationships along the way

that have truly blessed my life

and contributed to the grateful man of God I am today…

I honor you for your love

Many memories have truly warmed my heart by your beautiful smile

and your selfless acts of kindness…

I honor you for your sacrifice

Not many people including myself could have displayed the loyalty to the calling, and anointing you carry on your life…

I honor you for your strength

So many times when most would have given up, you kept on fighting…

I honor you for your courage

When many would have thrown in the towel, you continue to face your fears with grace…

I honor you for your voice

If it weren't for your encouraging words, I don't think I could have been as resilient as I am today…

Finally…

I honor you for your legacy

Your character has without a doubt contributed to the God-fearing, faithful, prayer warrior I am today…

Not only today, but I thank God for you always…

In my reflection, I see many beautiful pieces of you…

Forever in my heart, I gratefully honor you!

She is (My Mommy)

[#Poem #OdeToMother #Gratitude #MotherAndSon #Faith #Dedication #Love]

With a beautiful face
no one can ever replace
My mommy is an angel
forever full of grace
She helped me grow into a man
She helped me follow God's plan
Times were not always easy you see
Through the good days and the bad
she still kept her faith in me
Many broken promises
I once neglected her love

Yet she fought and prayed for my spirit

When push came to shove
She is my rock that is enough
She is my help when times are rough

She is my smile that brightens my day

She is my focus whenever I run astray

I love you so much and I'm proud of all you do

I don't know another person
who could have the strength
to pull through like you do
I'm sorry you had to wait so long
to receive a grateful son

Reflecting a loving mother who is so strong

I promise to do all I can to make it up to you

Our mother and son ministry
will one day come true
This I promise you

May God continue to bless all that you do

To my Wonder Woman mother

Beautiful, Amazing, Loved, and Faith filled

That's you
I love you

At the Alter

[#Poem #Surrender #Faith #Love #SetFree #Dedication #Christianity]

At the alter I have let go
Of the shame and guilt
I have always known
At the alter You can see
The grateful man
I long to be
At the alter I vow to You
To continue to shine
and be true to You
With all I do
At the alter I leave the pain
Your love has set me free
No longer bound in chains
At the alter I can finally see
You're the only One
Who can complete me
At the alter I hold Your hand

My loving Father
who always understands
At the alter I give my all to You
No matter how hard things get
I will live my best life for You
At the alter my love runs deep
Yes me
Your sometimes stubborn sheep
At the alter I hear You say
How much You love me
and You're proud of me today
At the alter I let go
of the bitterness and lies
Man will let me down
But Your love for me never dies

My Hero

[#Poem #OdeToMother #Love #Strength #Tribute #Inspiration]

M- It's for the millions of times I wish I had said I love you when I have the chance to

Y- For the many years, you have taken care of me when everyone else had given up on me while jumping ship

H- For the loving heart full of compassion you have shown to all that have confided in you

E- It's the empathy overflowing from my heart that will forever thank you for loving me as much as you do

R- It's for the true respect I now possess for others that you have always taught me to have no matter how hard it is to trust them

O- For obedience to our Lord and Savior Jesus Christ, that you have led me to follow Him

As a great example of leadership bringing all of this together has bonded us forever mom I love you thank you

True Friendship

[#Poem #Friendship #Loyalty]

True friendship multiplies the good in life, and subtracts the bad
Strive to have loyal friends for life
Without friends, life is like living on a desert island
To find one real friend in a lifetime is good fortune
To keep him is a true blessing

Thy Will be Done

[#Poem #Sin #Pain #Forgiveness #Purpose #Christianity]

In a world full of sin, persecution and broken promises, I've chosen to leave behind the salty tears of my secular, yet forgiven and crippled past. Where you see pain, and poverty beyond repair, God promises… perseverance, and prosperity to those who believe in His purpose for our destiny. I trade my troubles of this world to live a righteous life humbly under Your umbrella of mercy, and grace everlasting. Holy Spirit, lighten my path, one day at a time.
Like a bride faithfully committed to her groom, I died to self, letting go of this world. Promising to be still and remain loyal, constant, devoted, reliable, dependable, trustworthy, obedient, dedicated, and committed to You forever!

Treasure Out of Darkness

[#Poem #Faith #Christianity #Recovery #Addiction #Depression #MentalHealth #Relentless]

Lost in a sullen world, where there is no mercy, no grace and no hope. I feel the burden of the cross as my Father once did thousands of years ago. With Him only wanting my love, I expected nothing less than a perfect life. Selfishly destroying the life He has given me, I slowly start to fade away. Suffocating, addicted, brokenhearted, and starving for love, but looking at all the wrong places. I cry out to God wondering why bad things have to happen to good people? Be still, and know that I am the Lord of all circumstances, He has promised. Trust in me, my faithful servant, I will make you a beautiful treasure out of darkness. Shine on for the world to see, and never forget where I have brought you from!

No Other God

[#Poem #Dedication #Surrender #Tribute #Faith #Addiction #Sin #Depression #Deliverance Rated M]

Too many times we try to have it our way when it comes to walking in the spirit while trying to stay on a righteous path. Often more than not, we fall short of being blessed as we crawl through a web of entanglement and disillusion. It is in that moment, we realize God, and only God can save us from self-destruction.

No other God can love as deep as the symbolic Crimson blood He shed on the cross of Calvary to forgive my filthy sins. No other God can bring joy into my life after putting back together, shattered pieces of my broken heart.

No other God can peacefully calm the tsunami called sin that has single-handedly taken out many nations, including the one that promises "in God we trust."

No other God can gently nurse back to health the kicking, dope fiend that no one can trust.

No other God would kindly encourage the sad and lonely, unpopular kid no one seems to want to be around.

No other God can humbly display self-control in a world of greed and poverty, when you find out, you just won the lottery.

No other God can give you the power to endure long suffering after finding out the loss of your unborn child, while standing in the middle of your freshly painted nursery.

No other God can give you the patience to smile at the smoker whose cloud of smoke you just walk through on your way to the clinic to receive radiation treatment for the cancer that is slowly extinguishing your short lived life.

Finally, no other God can replace guilt and shame with goodness and selflessness. Against such things, there is no law. Those who belong to Jesus Christ have crucified, the sinful nature with its passions and desires. Since we live by the spirit, let us keep in step with the spirit, let us not become conceited, provoking, and envy each other. No longer eating the forbidden fruit from a tree that was never meant for me, I now produce good fruit from Your Holy Spirit.

Christ-like (Me)

[#Poem #Recovery #Addiction #Backslide #Surrender #Depression #Deliverence]

Separating myself from the crowd was the most advantageous, yet isolating decision that has come to pass in my new life of recovery. Sick and tired of the stench lingering from the vomit I had gone back to over and over again. I fall on my knees and reach for the sky. God hear my cry! A river of new life, flowing from my spiritually open eyes no longer ashamed, and reluctant to admit defeat. I was powerless over my transgressions, stemming from addiction, depression, and deceit. Once serving two masters, I rebuke the enemy as my trust, and faith in God have broken the chains of hypocrisy! It is only Christ you will see living in me.

Hide in My Heart

[#Poem #Death #Faith #Grace #Scripture #Freedom]

When the waves of death surrounded me, the floods of ungodliness made me afraid. Israel is swallowed up. Now it is among the gentiles, like a vessel, in which there is no pleasure. Most assuredly, I say to you, he who believes in me, the works that I do, He will do also and greater works than these will He do. Because, I go to my Father. But, each one of us, Grace was given according to Christ's gift. Therefore He says when He ascended on high, He led captivity captive, and gave gifts to men. Show your marvelous, loving kindness by your right hand. Oh, you who save those who trust in You, from those who rise up against them. Keep me as the apple of your eye. Hide me under the shadow of your wings. So I prophesied, there was a noise and suddenly a rattling and the bones came together bone to bone. And it shall come to pass in the last days says God that I will pour out my spirit on all flesh, and it shall come to pass that whoever calls on the name of the Lord, shall be saved! That if you confess with your mouth, the Lord Jesus, and believe in your heart that God has raised Him from the dead, you will be saved! Holy, holy, holy is the Lord God Almighty, who was and is to come! Behold my servant, who might I have chosen my beloved, and whom my soul is well pleased. For I know the plans I have for you, declares the Lord. Plans to prosper you and not to harm you, plans to give you hope and a future! I will give you the treasures out of darkness, and hidden riches of secret places that you may know that the Lord, who called you by your name, and the God of Israel, for where your treasure is, your heart will be also. Delight yourself in the Lord and He will give you the desires of your heart! And let us not grow weary while doing good, for in due season, we shall reap if we do not lose heart. Trust in the Lord, with all of your heart, and lean, not on your own understanding. In all your ways, acknowledge Him, and He shall direct your paths. Awake, you who sleep. Arise from the dead, and Christ will give you light. Let your light shine before men, that they may see your good works and glorify your Father in Heaven. So when Jesus had received the sour wine, He said, "It is finished!" and bowing his head, He gave up His spirit. The glory of the Lord shall be revealed, and all flesh shall see it together. For the mouth of the Lord has spoken! For I am already being poured out as a drink offering, and the time of My departure is at hand. I have fought the good fight. I have finished the race. I have kept the faith. Finally, there is laid up for me the crown of righteousness, which the Lord, the Righteous Judge, will give me on that day. And not to me only, but also to all who have loved His appearing!

Anointed Guardian Soldier

[#Poem #OdeToMom #Inspirational #Tribute #Dedication #BestFriend #MotherAndSon]

Courageous, beautiful, inspirational, faith-driven
She begins another day, helping others
with God's grace given talent, led by the Holy Spirit
Wholeheartedly she helps those who have given up
And feel like there is no hope left
Dedicated, spiritual, compassionate, benevolent
She fights against the enemy
with the two greatest weapons God has bestowed upon her;
the mighty word of God and prayer
Devoted, maternal, caretaking, empathetic
I could never ask for a better role model,
and best friend
She has been there for me all the days of my life
She has also spiritually adopted many
Broken and abandoned children
Making them feel special, wanted, and loved
Influential, heroine, mentor, advocate
She has accomplished more in her lifetime
Than I could ever dream of
She is my hero
She she is my strength
She is my heart
She is my best friend
She is my mom

Train a Child

[#Poem #Freedom #Surrender #Grace #Recovery]

Train a child to see love
through the eyes of gratitude
Reflection of a once broken heart
no longer having room
for unchanged behaviors
reaping a poor attitude
I finally let go
Not needing to put on a show
The final act is over
Curtain call
An encore of a Prodigal's persistence
Forecasting a new temperature
as the atmosphere has shifted
Turning tables once again
God says, "I'll do it again!"
Yes, my son
Proud to see grace
forever falling on your face
Recovery's relentless chase
has you in My embrace!

Jehovah (Help Me Fly)

[#Poem #Tribute #Dedication #OdeToMom #Faith #Recovery #MotherAndSon #Restoration #Deliverance]

Walking through the rain
Learning through the pain
Strong mother you have been
This world wouldn't be the same
If you hadn't introduced me
To His Holy name
Jehovah help me fly
Jehovah is the reason why
I try to make you proud
Mommy help the old me die
I promise to forever try
To be the man who
Never wants to make you cry
Drugs will never
Replace your hugs
I'd trade every wasted year
To take away your fear
Of never seeing your son

Clean up the mess
That caused you so much stress
That never allowed success

To fully reappear
As I look into the mirror
And shed a million tears
Jehovah help me please
Allow restoration to finally
Shift gears
Awaken my weary soul
To be the purpose-driven son
With the potential to
Unlock the chains
That once had me bound
This battle will finally be won!

In the Darkest Hour

[#Poem #EndTimes #Faith #Repentance #Surrender]

In the darkest hour, can you see my hand reaching out for your love?
In the darkest hour, I give you my hopes and fears
Knowing You can save us all
In the darkest hour, reality starts to set in
No more fairytales of a man who might come in the end
You are here as my faith has always trusted in You
In the darkest hour, who will you trust
To guide your broken life?
Believe in the One who will forgive your sin
No matter what you have done
In the darkest hour

Crush (Dear MJ)

[#Poem #Dedication #Romance]

Whenever I see you, my blood starts to rush
But how can I tell you, that I have such a crush?
This crush that I have
I can no longer hold within
Waiting for the one special day to come
when it is your love that I win
If it was truly meant to be, you will be mine in the end
So until the time comes, I can only pretend
and consider you as just a friend

Forever Yours (Poem for Jeremy)

[Poem #Dedication #Love #Romance]

As I look into your precious eyes
I see my own reflection
Painted rainbows fill the sky
You've shown me much affection
Butterflies and sweaty palms
My knees begin to shake
As tender kisses fill my heart
My soul is now awake
Please take me on a journey
Somewhere far away from here
It doesn't matter where we are
As long as you are near
So hold me close and don't let go
For we have yet to see
If I am truly meant for you
Then you are meant for me

I Want to be the One

[Poem #Dedication #Love #Romance]

I want to hold you in my arms
I want to kiss you in the rain
I want to wipe away your tears
And never cause you any pain
I want to be there when you laugh
I want to comfort you when you're sad
I want to be the one who will never make you mad
I want to tell you what I know
Though my heart I never show
All my secrets not to hide
I want to be the one who is always by your side
I want to be the strength that gets you through the day
I want to be your faith when you kneel down to pray
I want to be the key that will open up your heart
I want you always with me I hope we never part
So take me in your arms cause we have just begun
Let me be your baby boy
I want to be the one

Red Rose

[Poem #Dedication #Love #Romance]

Your love is like the reddest rose
So pure and sweet it always grows
Your eyes are like the stars at night
looking over me always, so warm and so bright
Your smile is so soft and sweet,
with the smoothness of your lips,
and the charm within your teeth
Love, I look forward to the joy of every day,
and through this poem, I would like to say
Our love is, and always will be that one red rose

Between the Sheets

[Poem #Dedication #Love #Romance Rated M]

The ice cream melts as it graces my tongue,
as does your flesh between the sheets.
The cotton candy quickly dissolves in my mouth,
feeling the body heat rises between the sheets
With a blow of my bubble gum,
we experience new, and exciting things
between the sheets
Between the sheets is where I crave you
My tooth aches

Doin' Me

[#Poem #Recovery #SelfLove #Freedom]

Now that you're behind me I feel so much stronger
Now that you're no longer in control
My true self can once again surface from the ashes of our relationship
We burned to the ground
Maybe now I can truly be risen for success
Recovering from the mess you have enabled me to become
I will live life on my own terms
I will be free
I'm doin' me

One Day Mom

[#Poem #OdeToMother #Apology #Forgiveness #Fear]

I fear the echo in the hallway
When I realize it's just me
I fear the smoke I've been inhaling
When your cancer is in stage three
I fear the tears that fill your eyes
When it was I who made them fall
I fear the disappointment and the lies
How could I have been the biggest hypocrite of them all?
So many times we come to judge
The ones who love us the most
How could I have burned so many bridges?
I ask the Father, the Son, and the Holy Ghost
I want to continue trying until you finally see
That I can earn your trust again
I promise mom one day you'll be proud of me

Don't Forget to Smile

[Poem #Love #Hope #Joy]

When you're feeling sad inside, and no one seems to care
Just wipe away your tears and know that I'll be there

Everyday Wounded Warrior

[#Poem #Recovery #Homosexuality #Surrender #Healing #Faith]

Broken and undone
This everyday wounded warrior
No longer seems to have any fun
Called to romanticize no one
When did life become so gray?
Was it when I decided not to be gay?
There is no greater love
I lay it all down
Yet my heart seems to still frown
From the pieces of glass
made up from my promiscuous past
Will celibacy and sobriety last?
I wanna stay true to the One who
saved my life
While loneliness eats away my soul
Cut my character defects with a knife
As I taste my tears I wonder
Am I just wasting years?
God help me see
If chasing You is really meant for me?
I never seem to stay true
as I continue to fall
and fail at everything I do
Help me through
Please God keep me
I wanna fully surrender to You
But I don't know how?
Please God
Help me pull through
The loneliness I feel
The struggle is real
Help me God
Please help me heal
This time for real

Who You See

[#Poem #Depression #Faith #Surrender #Trust #Purpose #Recovery #OdeToMother]

Too many times, I've tried to hide
the pain I felt inside…
Through the good times, and the bad…
This sometimes joyful, sometimes very sad soul had seen many demons, and dreams…
Somehow, he's still alive with a smile on his face…
To prove them all wrong, and make a positive impact on the human race…
His hopes have been trampled on at times, but his faith will forever stand…
He continues to hold on to God's sovereign hand…
PQ walks through life, as he tries to understand…
How to truly trust, and believe he can grow into a purpose-filled man…
Let his mom see her dream come to pass…
A son that fought for a clean and sober life at last!

Who's the Fairest of Them All?

[#Poem #Pride #Sin #Addiction #DrugUse #Sexuality Rated M]

Ride my coattails forever
In my shadow you will hide
I stole the bright light from you
Barely being a speck of glitter
twinkling in my eye
While I'm top shelf living
You're an expired coupon
barely surviving
I'm Rodeo Drive
You are Skid Row
My looks can hook anyone
More than a hit of
crack cocaine, or blow
I'm the high speed chase
Your the one night stand
no one wants to reface
Antique, and unique I'm a thrill
Your busted, disgusted, and over the hill
Vanity is my name
Narcissistic is my game
I will walk all over you
as you lick my Jimmy Chu shoe
I gather more compliments
Collected in my Louis Vuitton
You crawl out of a paper bag and hide
no one even notices your gone
Put me on a pedestal
how you wish you could be me
Your the leftover crumbs on the floor
Swept under the rug
so no one can ever see
Instead they're looking at me
The camera flashes
As I bat my eyelashes
Your the sad smeared mascara
running down my face
I wipe away your existence
You will never win first place
Just look at this face of perfection
as you can see
No one will ever adore you
and love you more than me
Just give up now
as you're just a temporary trend
I'll be here forever
My popularity will never end!

"On Solid Ground"

[#Poem #Prayer #Surrender #Faith #Surrender #Tribute]

Don't let my faith
become dead to doubt...
Discipline my prayer life
for Holy are You Lord
I scream and shout...
Wash me in Your blood
my Sovereign King...
Wash me in Your mercy
my sins are carried away
I'm now clean...
Here I Am Lord
oh I need You...
Here I Am Lord
take my hand...
Here I stand Lord
strong and willing...
Here I stand Lord
a changed man
trying to be the best I can...
Dream big
or don't dream at all...
Never doubt in the dark
what God has promised
in the light...
Never ask a question
where God has put an ending...
I serve Him through the eyes of faith
and not through the eyes of this world...
A dream fulfilled is a tree of life...
So I firmly plant my hope
and ambitions in His Eternal Garden
and know that He will bless my life
everywhere I go through the seed
that I sow, and through the love
I selflessly show...
Teach me to do Your will
so that I may please You
for You are my God
let Your good Spirit lead me
on solid ground...
This Christmas day I am so grateful
and proud to be your son
With this oath to You I say...
Happy Birthday Jesus...
I love You more, and more
every single day...
No longer having footprints
that walk away from Your love
My heart, and feet are planted firmly
On solid ground!

I Am (Proud Son)

[#Poem #Prayer #Surrender #Faith #Surrender #Tribute]

Tired of living
in the dimness of humanity
this once superficial
wounded warrior of the world
will no longer ride the coattails
of others success...
The time has come to rise up
Mighty Man of Valor
you are called and chosen
to lead this exclusive club
of hidden treasures...
No longer wondering
who's pulling strings above me
or dangling a carrot in front of me
I will not give my life up
for vain opportunity...
No longer seeking VIP social status
bright lights above my name
or considering carving my face
while starving to be famous
and selling out what morals I have left...
I realize, I don't need approval
apathy, or applause from anyone...
I am perfectly cut from the cloth
of my Creator...
I am an evangelistic tool from His shed...
I am His humble and faithful servant...
I am a man of righteousness and recovery...
I am a man of dignity and integrity...
I am a man of faith and forgiveness...
I am a man of peace and prosperity...
I am no longer prideful, but I am His proud son!

Forever Heal My Soul

[#Poem #Prayer #Surrender #Faith #Surrender #Tribute]

When you can't find the strength
to stand on your own
Know that the cross
has already promised you
a better life far beyond
the one you've always shown
You're a new creation
through Christ
so why do you believe
the lies of dream killers
and hope haters?
Count it all joy
and turn the other cheek
to those who persecute you
as they continue to fear your success
Forget gossip and rumors
Drama you no longer have contrail
From Genesis to Revelation
Your instructions fill my life
Hot coal from Heaven
cleanse my lips
and forever heal my soul

Letting Go

[#Poem #Prayer #Surrender #Faith #Surrender #Tribute]

At the altar
is where I can confess to You
All of the things I never thought
I'd put my loved ones through
As I come clean,
and You make me brand new
A life of freedom, I now live
I'm so grateful for blessing me
as much as You do
I let go of the hurt
I have carried for so long,
and the pain I've caused others
I've treated so wrong
I let go of addiction
that has kept me enslaved
Your Word is on my heart
I now have engraved
I let go of the pride
that has kept me from serving You
All of my selfish days
I never gave thanks for
anything that You do
Now broken in Your presence
is where I finally see
A humble man
and loving son
that You have called me to be

"Turn the Page"

[#Poem #Prayer #Surrender #Faith #Tribute]

Take my insecurities
Take my pride and pains
I'm more than ready now
for You to take my emotional chains
In order to turn the page,
this difficult season I must embrace
I kneel upon my knees,
as I seek Your Holy face
Through the storm
You've helped a little boy grow
Through the fire,
You've healed a once lost
and lonely soul
Through many tears,
You've changed this grateful life
It is through Your plans and purpose,
I will one day meet my beautiful wife

Better late than never,
I am learning how to be
the faithful man
You have called me to be
No longer spiritually bankrupt,
I put away childish things,
pick up my cross,
and march into destiny
with dignity as I sing
the praise song of victory
I am finally free to be me
Who You called me to be
Flying high
Peaceful, serene, and free

Keep Holding Me

[#Poem #Prayer #Surrender #Faith #Tribute]

When my heart starts aching
and I can't see you
When my nerves start shaking
and I can't feel you
Keep holding me so I can see
When the best of me
starts slowly fading
Every ounce I've given
You're remaking
Keep holding me so I can see
You're holding me
You carry me
through every season I'm facing
You carry me
every pain is erasing
You carry me
through every shame I'm embracing
My broken heart please carry me
When my burdens seem
to overtake me
When my shackles tighten
Your love will break them
The chains will fall

You love me all through it all
You're holding me
through every pill that I am taking
You're holding me
through every sip my heart's breaking
You carry me
through all the darkness I'm facing
My shattered heart
You carry me
You're holding me
through the smoke I'm inhaling
You're holding me
through every dollar I'm making
You carry me
through every smile that I'm faking
My wounded heart
keep holding me

Rest

[#Poem #Recovery #Prayer #12steps #Love #Faith #Forgiveness #Freedom #Healing]

To be a product of recovery is more than
a traditional prayer of serenity
Putting love into action means more
than lies of empty apologies
Twelve steps mean nothing
if you have cut off your own feet
with bitterness and resentments
Focus on the one set of footprints
to carry your baggage and brokenness
Fill your Spiritual cup
with compliments and kisses of truth
from your Higher Power
Avoid those who tell you that you are
anything less than loved and worthy
Humble yourself when you know you are wrong
Finally, give yourself a break
It's okay to love yourself
You don't have to walk this journey alone
Now look up
remember to breathe
and let the healing begin
God rest our souls

Grateful Man Here to Stay

[#Poem #Addiction #Recovery #Death #Depression #MentalHealth #Pride #Sexuality #Faith #Gratitude Rated M]

With a loaded chamber
crystal lifted the trigger to his head...
Another statistic marked by society
desperately wishing he were dead...
Tina broke apart his life
the pain he felt inside...
His heart shattered into a million pieces
because of selfishness, and pride...
Labeled a sexual deviant
a careless life he once lived...
Until Jesus broke the shackles free
and now all he wants to do is give...
No more broken promises
from a former ungrateful man...
He has been brought back to life
to faithfully follow into God's plan...
41 years of pain
have been washed away today...
Happy Birthday to this newly recovered life
a grateful man here to stay...

Falling Into Place

[#Poem #Surrender]

Sometimes things have to be broken, in order for things to be rebuilt into something beautiful.

Things aren't falling apart, they're falling into place! Just know that I am for you, not against you….

–God–

Prodigal Patrick Is No Longer

(A Son Who Has to Walk Alone) [Poem #Recovery #Dedication #Love #Tribute]

To not only my beloved brother in Christ…. You have been so much more…. You have been my accountability partner, my friend, and a spiritual father figure in my life…

When a family tied to blood has abandoned, and rejected me, you have proven throughout the years your loyalty to stay around and pour love, encouragement, and prayers into my life when I needed them most!

Love you….Many years gone by, before we finally met….But God's perfect timing proves that **Prodigal Patrick** isn't a son who has to walk alone…

In the Sand (Grow)

[#Poem #Recovery]

In the sand is where I grow...
In the sand is where You sow, and show a seed
how to fruitfully grow into a man...

Made New

[#Poem #Recovery]

"Don't ever let someone tell you, you're not the boy that you are…A new man in the making, a bright and shining star!"

Storms

[#Poem #Gratitude]

Be grateful for the storms in your life…
They reveal who your true friends are!

Roy G. Biv

[#Poem #Beauty #Reflection]

Red is the blood that is shed from all of the brave soldiers, who have died for our country
Orange is the sweet fruit that nourishes our bodies when we are in need
Yellow is the sun beating down on a hot summer's day
Green is the grass in which children like to play and roll around in all day
Blue is the sky that is full of beautiful creatures who know how to fly
Indigo is the color of the sweater I gave my mom on her birthday
Violet is the delicate iris that is blooming ever so beautifully in the garden
Now ask yourself, who is Roy G. Biv?

Battlefields and Butterflies

[#Poem #Transformation]

This battlefield I've been trudging across is too dangerous to save you anymore
Who is going to rescue me when I reach full capacity?
When I call for help, will you be my hero?
Will you ignore me?
Or will you be the one I need rescuing from?
Sometimes I wish I were a butterfly, having the ability to transform myself
from a slimy creature into something beautiful that can just fly away

Christmas Decorations (Helen's Poem)

[#Poem #Tribute #Dedication #Love]

As the light crystal snowfall graces, the crusted autumn leaves winter is drawing near

As you see the enormous smile on my face, I can see how very excited you are that Christmas is almost here

We make our way to the garage. What treasures can be found?

As we search our way through the top of the pile

We then come across many things we haven't seen in a very long while

As we hurry in to fight the cold air, we throw a log on the fire and begin to put up Christmas decorations everywhere

Radiant and luminous lights warm up this cozy place

With Christmas decorations, memories of Christmas with you can never be replaced!

Stepping Out

[#Poem #Purpose]

Nothing will ever fulfill you until you're stepping into what God has called you to do…Put doubts underneath your feet where they belong, and step out in faith!

PART 2:
THE BOUND AND BROKEN HEART

'You will seek me and find me, when you seek me with all your heart.'

JEREMIAH 29:13

My Psalm

[#Poem #Surrender #Backslide #Recovery #Christianity #Sin #DrugUse #Addiction]

When your heart feels paralyzed, and you're stuck, call upon the name of Jesus to carry you through your hard times, and stop depending on false hope and superstitious luck. Tired of feeling like a plastic bag blowing in the wind, time has slipped away as I have not so discreetly gone astray from God's plan, and selfishly fallen back into rebellious, and redundant sin. Spun, out of control, losing my mind isn't so fun anymore. Flying high in the mile high, I start to come down and reality begins to sink in. God has called me to rise up, and save souls, starting with my own. As I let go of childish things, I exterminate any possible connection to the toxic shards of broken glass I have idolized to numb myself from being a real man. With a one-way ticket in hand, I pack my bags and head to Albuquerque. Burning the bridge to my Egypt, and reopening my once encrypted heart to be healed, and mended by the Holy One, who will carry me to the finish line. With the heart of David, the favor of Joseph, the courage of Gideon, and the faith of Job, I am unstoppable, and will forever be known as God's loyal and faithful servant! Resting in the center of my Lords safekeeping palm, this is the promise of my own personal Psalm.

So Addicted

[#Poem #ExplicitLanguage #Surrender #Backslide #Recovery #Christianity #Sin #DrugUse #Addiction #Homosexuality #EatingDisorder Rated M]

Take a look at the heroin junkie
Does he have the strength to stand alone?
By alone, I mean, not having to depend on a quick fix to "get well"
If I were to open your medicine cabinet,
how many scripts and pills will I find versus how many you actually need?
How many big-time gamblers will you come across in Vegas daily spending away their life savings, while still wanting to hit the "big one?"
Online, you can find the young sex-addicted twink
cruising Adam4Adam for his next conquest and bed-post notch to fly high with while slamming crystal meth at a sex party
In a small, southern country town a teen is caught by her obese mother,
nearly eating in an entire bag of Oreo cookies in one sitting
While down the road, poor young girl sheds tears and pounds
while suffering from anorexia and bulimia as Cosmopolitan Magazine
has mind fu*ked her into believing that rail thin is hot
and a girl with meat on her bones is not
These are the addictions faced by society
I challenge each and every single one of you,
instead of criticizing yourself for a flaw you may have
See something beautiful about yourself, and complement it daily
Trade a nasty habit for a positive affirmation instead
Pray to God daily to tear down those strongholds that hold you in bondage,
while keeping you in captivity
Free yourself, and become addicted to God instead!

Deliverance From Suffering

[#Poem #Alcoholism #Addiction #DomesticViolence #Abuse #Death Rated M]

He came home one night and staggers
through the front door
With vodka on his breath, she tries hard to ignore
An unfamiliar scent of perfume lingers through the air
Like a swift knife through her heart, she knows he's having an affair
He begins to yell and cause a fight
She starts to pack her things
She slowly moves toward the door
As he grabs a bat, and fiercely swings
So innocent and fragile, she tried not to let go
At her funeral, we mourn as I sit in the front row
She was such a free spirit, too hard not to love
Though she suffered a lot, I know she smiles
from up above

Eternal Flame

[#Poem #Depression #MentalHealth]

Enlightened by the beauty of the candles, flame
I'm reminded of the presence of my eternal soul
Wondering where I want to go?
Currently, I feel empty, and saddened as the candles wax trickles down
I can taste my salty tears stream down my face
What was once presented as everlasting beauty
Is now seen as self destruction
The aroma of fresh flowers slowly fade away
As does my hopes and dreams of becoming a healthy and somewhat normal person
Tomorrow's another day as an opportunity to shine
Joy will one day be mine!

Project Sanity

[#Poem #Relapse #Addiction #CoDependency #DonesticViolence #DrugUse Rated M]

Today is the day I can finally say that I am free to walk alone

Sadly, my own mother, and guardian has given up on me for good this time (or so I think)

And she's always good for her word

Though I can understand, reasoning behind her tough love, I can never do enough to please her, as she expects perfection

I have let my favorite Wonder Woman down, as well as my hero, and my best friend

It all started when I met the man I adored, and love of my life (so I thought)

Till you came along, life had no excitement, and was quite boring with not enough meaning behind my unknown existence

I craved more

Instead, you turned me into a whore

True empathy from my heart, thanks both of you for helping me finally start to grow up.

I used to feel like quite a celebrity thinking back on all of my plastic acquaintances, and fans I would idolize on my "fakebook" wall

Before it became my current journal, therapy, and "faithbook"

Now I realize the only ones that count are my true friends, you know who you are (but, where did they go?)

Since my life has seemed to spiral out of control, I have lost hope, and the ability to see through the lens of love and life

Most of my time lately has been spent on losing myself in the drug,

that keeps me numb from reality, and from mentally breaking down

At the same time, I need to come to realize that my poor choices lately have caused me to reap what I sow, while wreaking havoc and consequence

Now that I have plenty of excitement, a.k.a. drama in my life, I am just as miserable as I was while living the simple kind of life

There seems to be no win and win on either side of the spectrum

When will I be sane and stable again?

Will there ever be a sense of clarity in my life?

When will I receive my happy ending?

Sigh…

Till then, this has been my edge of evolution, and hope for my future's project sanity, and success.

Poem for Zack

[Poem #Romance #Abuse #CoDependency]

I love the way you smile
I hate the way you lie
I love the way you laugh
I hate it when you cry
I love when I amuse you
I hate when you abuse me
I love all the cool things that you can do
When you're not too busy, hurting and controlling me
I love to sing you love songs
I hate it when you call me hurtful names
I love it when you give me flowers and candy
I hate it when you play mind games
I love that you're my best friend
I hate that you're my worst enemy
I once would have loved to be with you until the end
I'd hate to live life without you by my side
I love that I love you
I hate that I hate you
I love that we have had some of the most amazing times together
I hate that we have done some of the most hurtful things to each other
I love that you're my hero
I hate that you never saved me
I love that you're the greatest love I have ever had
I hate that this is sadly the end
Goodbye, my friend

Tragic Love Story

[#Poem #ExplicitLanguage #DomesticViolence #CoDependency #DrugUse]

Don't know why you still affect me, and do the things you do?
Don't know why you still infect me, when you know that we are through?
Don't know why I should believe you, after all the lies you told?
Don't know why I still adore you, when you treated me so cold?
Don't know why I let you in, for my heart you would mistreat?
Don't know how I could begin, to worship the ground you walk on, as I kiss your dirty feet?
You don't know how to choose your life, as Dr. Jekyll or Mr. Hyde?
I refuse to be in your life again, so go and find yourself a Bonnie you deviant Clyde!
I no longer want to see the way you view the human race.
I no longer want to feel the pain from your fist across my face.
No longer let you be, the one who continues to do me wrong.
I will move on with my life again, you have fucking hurt me for way too long!
Don't ever call me again, for you will never see
The bruises and the scars within my heart, I have finally set you free!
Like a dog that licks its vomit, maybe he might take you back.
For you have lost the one you claim to love, and no I'm never coming back!
I thank God in heaven, from above, He deserves all the glory.
He has finally healed my pain, and heart, putting an end to this tragic love story!

Overdue Overdose (Bullshit Stew)

[#Poem #ExplicitLanguage #DomesticViolence #CoDependency #DrugUse]

Now that you're finally out of my life, I can be myself without having to sensor any part of who I am, while running away in fear you might hit me again.

I'm surprised you never liked to wear muscle shirts, because you sure the fuck are a wife beater!

Will your chicken shit attacks come for me once again by all of your false accusations, fucked up dreams, and bullshit stew?

Funny how you can only gain control over me through your transparent lies that fall from your shit smelling breath, yet you say you love me so, promising never to lie, or to let go.

Pretty ironic don't you think?

Just because you're too big a coward to handle your own consequences, doesn't give you the right, nor the power to think you are bigger than God.

His plans are already intact, and no matter how hard you try to ruin my life, you will fall flat on your face each time.

My best advice to you is simply this, get over it, get over me, and stay the fuck away from me.

Because I've finally had an overdue overdose of your bullshit stew!

Sick and Tired (Betrayal Lingers)

[#Poem #ExplicitLanguage #DomesticViolence #CoDependency #DrugUse]

I'm so sick and tired of being sick and tired

I'm tired of being rewired each time you change your mind of who I am supposed to be, at any particular time

I'm tired of your fucked up outbursts

I'm tired of you hating me

I'm tired of the residue of your shallow behavior, at the bottom of my shoe that I still have to walk in daily

I'm tired of still feeling betrayed, causing me to encrypt my hurting heart

I'm tired of telling everyone that I'm OK, when I'm really not

I'm tired of feeling sorry for myself, when it was I who took you back time and time again

I'm tired of succumbing to the realization that I'm nothing more than a hopeless, homeless, junkie

I'm tired of being your shackled slave

I'm tired of the days accumulating, before I can see the light of freedom, and a normal day

I'm tired of accepting the person, who doesn't want me to grow in any kind of way

I'm tired of feeling suffocated by your destructive ways

I'm tired of waiting for you to change, when I should be focusing on changing myself

I'm tired of being stupid enough to believe that you could about face

But most of all, I'm sick and tired of loving you, and for you treating me with such disgrace!

Abomination of Love

[#Poem #ExplicitLanguage #DomesticViolence #CoDependency #DrugUse]

All of the pain that I'm holding within
is drowning my soul and destroying my heart
Never would have thought it could hurt so bad,
still I knew I loved you from the very start
I know that no one's perfect,
and we have yet to see that the beauty
of becoming one was never meant for you and me
Sheltered in the corner of this one-way relationship,
I now rise from upon your feet.
Never been afraid to admit defeat,
you must now pay for all of this deceit.
For that now my words will be heard
in such a way that may offend you
Because believe me love, every word that I say is true
They say we're not compatible, and that we would not last
My first impression was the same, because we moved so fast
To always be the one who would always hold your hand
I always made your dinner, your wish was my command
I'm sick and tired of a relationship
based on whatever you say is whatever we do.
It is now time for my feelings to finally come across to you,
and for my judgment to be heard through.
Fallen from the pedestal in which you were once placed
Always knowing you were afraid of heights, you must now be erased
Caring and respect are only two things that you lack.
So pack your shit, hit the road, and never come back!

Salted Wounds and Painted Moons

[Poem #BreakUp #Heartache]

Once upon a time you seemed quite friendly
and quite normal
You always knew just how a win me over
that was a time when the stars, and the moon
had lined up just right, and painted a pleasant picture for our success
Now that I have had a taste of the salt,
you now throw in my open wounds,
and hurt you have brought into my world
I can never allow us to happen again
I should've known happiness was too good to be true
You are just a dirty, old wolf hidden in sheep's clothing.
Sad, but true.

I Thought About You Today

[#Poem #Romance #BreakUp #Goodbye]

I thought about you today….I missed you without hating you….I chose to block out the noise from other people's opinions….I trust God is taking care of you…. Remembering that one moment of pure happiness February 14th after dinner made me smile….I wasn't prepared for this kind of pain….I'm sorry for giving you my heart, when it was never meant to give away….Today, I choose recovery over suffering and revenge….I may have lost my job, my money, my confidence in materialism, and the best friend I trusted, and truly never knew….But I have gained something even greater, I have found a new purpose to love, live, and laugh….You were my drug, and my remedy….You were the perfect idol that should have never been placed on a pedestal…. Today, I still grieve what could have been….More importantly, I embrace sacrifice, and suffering to chase God once again through obedience….Live well my friend…

XO, PQ

Fear of Bliss and Fear of Loving You

[#Poem #Romance #BreakUp #Goodbye]

How can misery love company
I often seem to say
You somehow appear to hurt me
In every possible kind of way
I gave you my heart
I gave you my trust
I even gave you control
Yet you took me for granted and made me run
And now you're after my soul
Fear of bliss and fear of loving you
Fear of our failed success
And fear you'll love me too
Fear of complete solitude
And fear of humble pie
I fear our future unknown
I fear you will make me cry
I've tried to be strong
I've tried to rebuild
I've tried to be just like you
But somehow I find the more that I try
The less you seem to do
How do I know as real as it seems
That the love we share is true?
So many hopes and so many dreams
Have been crushed because of you
Fear of bliss and fear of leaving you
Fear such lack of success
And fear you'll leave me too
Fear of complete solitude
And fear of humble pie

I can almost hear them saying now
"How does he put up with this guy?"
So many lies have come to pass
My happy endings prevented
With your sociopathic ways
Another character you've invented
I hate to love you and love to hate you
I am the lie above all your lies
Showing no signs of slowing down
Another plan we must devise
Fear of bliss and fear of changing you
Fear of no such success
And fear you'll change me too
Fear of complete solitude
And fear of humble pie
I fear how much you have taught me
I fear we might give it another try
Fear of bliss and fear of praise too
Fear of brightness and fear of positive attitudes
Fear of bliss and fear of compassion too
Fear of wholeness and fear of wisdom is true
Fear of bliss and fear of striving too
Fear of stability and fear of flying with you
Fear of feeling complete for complete you make me feel
And fear of the hearts we will break by seeing our love shine through
Fear of bliss and fear of hurting you
Fear of our success and fear you'll hurt me too
Fear of complete solitude
And fear of humble pie
I fear the many times we can't erase
I fear we may never know why?
Please don't let me die and leave me alone to cry

Moral Bankruptcy

[#Poem #Addiction #DrugUse #Depression #StrongSexualContent #ExplicitLanguage Rated M]

I was falling apart when I gave you my heart
The grave you'd dig for me
My battle wounds and a million scars will tell you my history
So many tears have hit the ground during many lonely nights
I tried to love you through the pain but all we did was fight
You'd constantly feed me lies claiming everything you did was right
But I disappeared more and more as addiction made me lose sight
You'd ask where did he go?
No one knows how many times I had to fake the painted smile on my face
Every minute wasted on you was a mistake
In the clouds another day wasting my life away
In the clouds is where I stay to numb myself today
I pick up my phone when I'm alone this pain is real you see
To rub one out or reach for him is all I know how to be
In the clouds another day wasting my life away
In the clouds is where I stay to numb myself today
Grindr men knock at the door I want more
Yes, I have become a filthy whore
These races have grown tired I no longer want to run
The bag is gone I'm spun again will this curse ever be done?
No more clouds let's get to the point out of control
Endless sexual energy
I pray to God to end my life or finally set me free
I choose to be free
No more pain you see
Self inflicted by me the broken man I use to be
Thank You Lord for rescuing me
I am free
I am free
Broken no more

I'll Be (Who's Loving Me?)

[#Poem #Romance #BreakUp #Goodbye]

You said you loved me back then
Said you would never hurt me again
Guess what
You let me down once again
Said you would always be in my life
So why did you stab me in the back with a knife?
I heard you once had a wife
Why you gotta have a new life without me in it?
You said he was just a friend
The part of being next to you I never knew
So why do they get to see
What I never got to see in you?
I'll be your shelter through all the rain
Who's loving you when it should be me?
It's so unclear why can't you see it now?
I'll be your soldier through everything
You never locked me outside the door
Who's loving me why can't it be you now?
You never really showed me your pain
Did you ever really feel what I felt the same?
Please let me in once again
Does he know you gave me your life?
Does she know that I have your life?
Be my best friend once again
The part of being next to you I always knew
If you let me hold you in your arms I promise to never stop loving you
I'll be your healer when you're in pain
If I choose to love you will you love me the same?
It's very clear we can both see it now
I'll be your power and everything if you let me wear your diamond ring
I'm healing you and you're healing me
It's very clear when we both can see
Who's loving you?
Why can't it be me once more?

When U (Left Without a Trace)

[#Poem #Romance #BreakUp #Goodbye]

See me as your lifeline
Or seek me for revenge
See me as a tragedy
Just don't play me pretend
I justify my triggers
When you appear as very nice
Freedom never lasts
When rejected more than twice
How can I be judged
for bad decisions from my past?
When you have never been
a loyal friend that doesn't last
When God has given grace
to save me from a broken place
You erase my Godly reputation
As you run away without a trace
Remember the mess you made
by causing me to fall
Who is the villain this time?
Only God's justice
will tell us once and for all

Don't Cry

[#Poem]

No one is truly worth your tears
The one that is, will never make you cry.

Fly Back Home (Super Save Me)

[#Poem #OdeToMother #OdeToFather #Homosexuality #Addiction #EatingDisorder #Romance #BreakUp #Goodbye]

How many times will it take me to recognize my fatal mistakes, before it's too late to save the world. As she flies around in her invisible plane, constantly saving others, I can only wonder what kind of woman can defend her Christianity while battling cancer at the same time?

I can only imagine what kind of man can stand up for his sexuality, or non sexuality while fighting HIV, drug addiction, being homeless, and an eating disorder? With your x-ray vision, can you see inside my broken heart, and would I care to see what's inside of yours, or do my scornful words still affect the way you promised to save my life, as I would gladly take a bullet to save yours.

You don't have to be Superman, so quit trying. Will this golden lasso of truth and honor stop all of your lying? You always said you'd be my hero, yet when I think of the number of times we have saved each other, I can't count past zero. Why must you be my kryptonite? I just want my best friend back, and wounded hero in my life. Why must you insist on winning every losing fight? Free me from destabilization, I'm not ready to say goodbye just yet.

I hate that you're not here with me. I hate that I can't make you see that I still adore you, even though I don't want to at times. I hate that I don't trust the man that's been so unfair to me, yet when I relive all that I've been suffering from, I know that no matter what you'll always have my back, as I'll have yours in return. I hate that you can't trust me, I promise I have nothing to hide. I love that you still love me, it keeps me from dying inside.

I'm not asking for a man with superhuman powers, or for you to leap tall buildings just to bring me flowers. I'm not asking for your wealth, or for you to save the human race. I just want you to come back in my life again, with that beautiful smile upon your face. We all deserve another chance for truth, justice, and the American Way. So fly back home where you belong, and let our love save the day.

Love Impossible

[#Poem #Romance #BreakUp #Goodbye]

I'm so tired of saying goodbye, trying hard to keep just one in my life forever seems impossible.
The more I give myself another chance to love, the harder I fall on my face while breaking my heart once again.
Maybe I'm not made for loving?
Maybe I'm too hard to hold onto?
Until I can truly love myself, there is no point in anyone else trying to love me.
Love seems impossible.

Any Given Some day (tweaked out again)

[#Poem #Romance #BreakUp #Goodbye #DrugUse #ExplicitLanguage #StrongSexualContent #Abuse #MentalHealth Rated M]

Looking back on the days of you and I,
I wonder was there ever a private moment captured between us?
All I ever wanted was a normal relationship with you, not some video recorded,
and documented disastrous train wreck,
viewed by all who cared to watch it.
You always seemed to care more for your electronics than me
I wonder if our livestream has had more hits than Madonna has had in her entire career?
In the end, I was a bit extreme when it came to censoring all of my feelings,
and what I'd say around you
It's as though I was like Britney Spears being chased down by the paparazzi
Then I wonder
What was I suddenly famous for?
Oh yeah being your whore
All of these cameras pointed at me, and no clue why?
Hell, I think I've had my photo taken more than Paris Hilton these days
Difference is
At least that bitch is getting paid
Are you secretly an agent spy, and I the unknowing spy's other half?
Or are you from another country, a foreign leader, or president
and I your unknowing so-called first lady?
At least, give me a fair warning before the flash bulbs go off again
Making sure the cameraman at least captures my good side
on the other side of his lens
Does this outfit match my shoes?
Or will I be wearing anything at all?
Seems even the porn stars on the internet can pass for someone looking just like me
Is this real? Is this really happening or am I going crazy?
Fame isn't everything it's cracked up to be
Or maybe it's the drugs clouding up my memory?
Please save me once again from "wacko island," as you'd call it
I'm tweaked out again, and need some serious sleep and nourishment
As I shut down my paranoia, I will fall out so that I can regain
my "normal" state of mind once again
Then again, what is normal right?
This has been another episode of Quezada's Crazy life on any given someday
good night signing out.

Shameless Bag Whore *(Fucking Junkie)*

[#Poem #Romance #BreakUp #Goodbye #DrugUse #ExplicitLanguage #StrongSexualContent #Abuse #MentalHealth Rated M]

As my life disintegrates into the cloud of smoke blown from upon these lips, I can only wonder…Is it too late to start living? Or too early to start dying? Walking dead I have become again overnight…As I lurk in the shadows, while turning tricks between the sheets for another shot into Nirvana I fly so high…Numbing myself from my own personal hell, I dwell beneath the cracks and filth of society barely existing…I can hardly breathe an honest breath, as I nearly choke on my own vomit when realizing what I have become a fu*%ing junkie! Why can't I quit this euphoric, yet extremely demonic substance I've asked myself a thousand times over and over again? Who is in control of these transparent dangling strings this week? Purgatory never seemed to suit my trendy sense of style, I fly first class all the way…question is…Which master do I serve? The angel in my heart, or the devil in my head? Church on Sunday morning, or Adam4Adam Friday night instead? Hmmm… All of these choices in my head…Yet, my heart only has room for one particular man's love in my bed…Oh well for now, another day of party n play, as I load my rig with another forty cent shot today…I seem to lose my reputation somewhere between the bathhouse, and the bookstore on East Colfax along the way…Colfax, you say? No I'm not a hooker, I just play one on TV…Laugh out loud! Will responsibility ever seem to see the light of day? Or will AIDS, and Hepatitis C be the death of me, as most statistics seem to say? All work and no play make for a very boring lifestyle, I always say…Meanwhile, as the normal man pays bills daily, I'm kicking it with my homegirl Tina, she's my baby! Hell, the only "Bill" I know is the name of the contact in my cell phone…He's the dopest dope man that rules the world…A man with shiny crystals in a bag for his well-known gold-digging fag! My mouth waters for more…Someone please help this shameless bag whore! Give me more!

Devil In My Veins

[#Poem #Romance #BreakUp #Goodbye #DrugUse #ExplicitLanguage #StrongSexualContent #Abuse #MentalHealth Rated M]

Help me I'm drowning
in a sea of regret
This brittle body of bones
can no longer love
without an offensive threat
With the tip of a needle
I shoot the devil into my veins
Nothing but a compulsive addiction
to meaningless sex remains
I fly so high between the sheets
as I use Grindr
to pick up random men
from the streets
Property of none
I seek to devour
Another perfect 10
to surrender all power
As the ice cracks back
we blow clouds of lust
into the air
With porn and poppers we soar
Watching our once driven lives
now dimmed by despair
As the Reaper continues
to knock at the door
All I can think of is
I want more
Death is in store
as my Spirit is at war
The party is now over
and I'm alone on the floor
Yet I want more
I still want more

Waste of Talent

[#Poem #Addiction #Death Rated M]

With all of the signs of a promising life that seem to say
Stay away from alcohol before a life ends today
To be so stubborn not to let go
To nearly lose your life
To have no control
To not have a choice in which road to take
Four friends take the wheel before they think or hesitate
With their future not in mind
Yet in their hand they cheers with beers
To make a foolish decision
How can one possibly understand?
The wheels begin to shake
Their bodies very frail
How to end this nightmare
They now face death or jail
The car spins around
As they realize what they've done
Well now it is too late
Another tragedy has won
The sirens start to sound
They know what they must do
Surrender to the one
Who will help pull them through
They pray to God above to put their soul at ease
To cure their alcoholism and rid from this deadly disease

Vanity

[#Poem #EatingDisorder #Depression #MentalHealth #Addiction Rated M]

"How great you look!" Friends and family say
It's all of the weight that I've wasted away
Tired of always being so fat
I begin to lose the weight hoping some day
Maybe I can look like that
Just because I appear to be thin
People don't see the pain that I feel within
With my self-esteem feeling so low
I lose the weight in a way that you may not know
I eat very small portions every now and then
Wondering how to survive, I never want to eat again!

Mirror Mirror

[#Poem #EatingDisorder #Depression #MentalHealth #Addiction Rated M]

Mirror...mirror on the wall
Who's the most prideful of them all?
Wasting away, or stuffing my face
I am longing to erase
The troubled space
In my head
I seek to embrace
More compliments of
Another superficial dopamine replace
Such a coward
I now trace
How could I come to this place?
Of vanity yet insecure race
Binge and purge
No more food do I want to taste
Yet I can't stop
So much food I waste
Still I choose to shove more
In my face
Please take me far from
This addicted state
Of the anorexia and bulimia
I want to embrace
Because I can't see
The superficial space
This lie I have come to believe
Of the eating disorder
I continue to chase
Because I can't see
A beautiful face
Because I choose to replace
Love for myself within an empty space
I try to seek a safe place
Of a medium normal
Will I ever fulfill my size
Of a desirable waist?
I look at all the perfect bodies
I'll never be able to fake
The waiter comes to my table
Can I take your order?
I say
Check please
No more lonely party of one
Will this eating disorder make of me
I am free
To be me
Any size of body you see
Because beautiful lies
Inside of me

Master of Intimidation

[#Poem #Addiction]

As the vodka quickly dissolves the ice,
I think to myself wouldn't it be nice to have just one more drink?
All of my friends think that I've had too much.
Funny, I don't think so.
Hardly intimidated by this drug, I soon become out of control.
Barely able to walk, I stumbled to the ground, as I hang my face over the toilet bowl.
Intoxicated by so much vodka,
I'm poisoned by this deadly drug.
Not knowing anything that happened the night before,
I wake up ill, lying on this vomited rug.

My Biggest Fear

[#Poem #Fear #EatingDisorder #Rejection #Addiction #DomesticViolence Rated M]

My fear is to be fat again
My fear is not to see
My fear is you'll find someone
Who is more capable than me
My fear is to be abandoned
My fear is not to be loved
My fear is to be unstable
And rejected by God's love
I fear I will never leave you
As you have hurt me through and through
I fear there is no point in anything that I do
I fear I will be judged for the pedestal is too high
I fear the alcohol on your breath
I fear how many times you have made me cry
I fear the swelling on my face
I fear the drugs I have embraced
I fear I ruined mom's life
I fear I'll never have a wife
Why am I so different?
I guess I'll never see
The hopes and dreams I once had
And why my biggest fear is me?

To Walk on Broken Glass

[#Poem #Depression #DrugUse #Addiction #Rejection #Fear]

As I wake up in the morning and stumble out of bed
I feel like a shackled slave, who is only allowed one crust of bread
It is the dawn of a new day, yet another day that I dread
I take a look in the mirror and wonder where my life has been led?
Every wrinkle on my face
Every teardrop in my eye
To walk on broken glass
I can only wonder why?
Wanting to pick up the pieces
That I have swept under my bed
For the life that I once had
Is just an illusion in my head
As I wake up in the morning and stumble out of bed
I turned to drugs and alcohol
"Be careful," mama said
With daddy not around he's never shown me love
Depression got the best of me
I pray to God above
Every wrinkle on my face
Every teardrop in my eye
To walk on broken glass
I can only wonder why?
Wanting to pick up the pieces

That I have swept under my bed
For the life that I once had
Is just an illusion in my head
The path that I have chosen seems so dark and cold
Not knowing how to fly again
A failure I've been told
I once was known as innocent
And driven for success
I pray to God to ease my mind,
and calmly put my soul to rest
Every wrinkle on my face
Every teardrop in my eye
To walk on broken glass
I can only wonder why?
Wanting to pick up the pieces
That I have swept under my bed
For the life that I once had
Is just an illusion in my head
Picking up the pieces
That I have left under my bed
For the life that I once had
Is still an illusion in my head

Beneath the Bridge

[#Poem #Depression #Mental Health]

I feel sick sick to my stomach
This chronic depression, I'm presently suffering inflicts
acid into my system that seeps away at my soul
Leaving no room for confidence, nor anything to possibly look forward to
This confined desperation consumes my hopes and dreams of becoming anything
more than just an infatuated junkie
Seeking love and companionship, I dwell beneath the bridge
The bridge society tramples on my very own self existence
As a tear hits the gravel, I realize that I am nothing

Anointed Sinner

[#Poem #Sin #DrugUse #Addiction #Faith #Hope #Surrender]

It doesn't matter how many good deeds we perform in a lifetime.

When it comes down to it, in the end we're all sinners.

So many days I wake up and ask myself why am I so special?

How can I be one of God's chosen soldiers, when I still live my life foolishly, and sin.

How can I call myself saved when I feel lost daily?

What kind of Christian brother am I to praise the Lord Sunday mornings in church, while healing new track marks up and down those hypocritical and guilty arms?

I cry out for help and forgiveness sincerely, but what good is it asking for assistance with something that you're not truly ready to fully sacrifice?

When it comes down to it, in the end, I would gladly do anything and everything

I can to help a loved one into God's kingdom, even if it meant nearly losing myself in the process.

These things that are constantly in the back of my mind

are the many questions I have asked myself, and others time and time again.

Those supposed Christians constantly judge who I should and shouldn't love

has no merit in anyone else's life other than my own.

Stop being religious, and start being relational.

I have faith that God will ultimately guide me onto the path

that He has mapped out for my life.

I have accepted His unconditional love.

I have relented. Turned away from a lifestyle that I no longer want to be a part of,

and I'm prepared to dedicate all of my love to Him above anything else.

I am His anointed sinner saved by Grace!

"Pride" (Before the Fall...)

[#Poem #Sin #Pride #DrugUse]

I am the one
who selfishly took
the elderly woman's place in line
at the grocery store...
I am the one
who lied on my resume
to get the job I didn't deserve...
I am the one
who stole
mom's rent money
to score a fix...
I am the one
who has
all of the right answers
at exactly the right time...
I am the one
you wish you could be...
I am the handsome one...
I am the intelligent one...
I am the perfect one...
I am the selfish one...
I am the one
who will lie, cheat, and manipulate
my way in any situation
to get what I want...
I will step on your toes
stab you in the back
and stop at nothing
that will keep me from achieving
ultimate success...
You can either love me
as your best friend
or hate me
as your worst enemy...
I am Pride!

"The Backslider (Fallen)"

[#Poem #Backslide #Sin #Depression]

With nothing to show the promising
of a purpose-filled life worth living
he allowed routine, and sinful desires
take over...
As he walks away from the Healer
he has sadly chosen to fall from grace
and reinfect his life with havoc
and chaos once again...
Fighting a losing battle to stress
and his emotions
he gives into his weak flesh...
Ignoring conviction, and his mother's
tears
he finds himself hopelessly depressed
at the bottom of an empty bottle
and broken with no sense of dignity, or
hope...
Smelling the familiar and enticing
stench of vomit in the air
this old dog in filthy rags
has gone back into the world...
Back to the days of his old ways...
Back to allowing bad feelings
overcome his faith in the One
who will never hurt him...
Back to selfishness, over sacrifice...
Back to slavery, over salvation...
Once full of hope
this evangelist has lost his fire
and desire to lead others to the truth
as he has fallen for the lies
of the enemy dressed in a clever
disguise
called, "normal, and everyday
comfortable life"...
Nearly losing all hope
he cries himself to sleep wondering....
Is this the end of me???

Don't Bite (the Apple)

[#Poem #Sin #Backslide #DrugUse #Addiction #StrongSexualContent #ExplicitLanguage Rated M]

They say an apple a day
will keep the doctor away
But wasn't it the apple
that began sin
on the very first day?
Pipes, and needles,
pills, and bottles galore
Hitting up the dope man
while on your way
to pick up another whore
More selfish Prime
deliveries to your door
From the Amazon store
When you can't pay your rent
Yet you still order more
Greed has got you
Stealing pennies
From the poor
For your 5G network
prison platform
Yet you still want more
No not me
I refuse to let this world
continue to corrupt me
Still you choose to dive in
this world of confusion
Where our constitution
is now an illusion
Where Adam and Eve
become Adam and Steve
Millions of aborted babies
women will leave
and not conceive
Please believe
the end of dark days
we will see
If you put your trust in Him
not me
Masked, and vaccinated
When I'm lost at sea

Please help me
I'm drowning in vanity
in a world of "Fakebook"
Self seeking sanity
Tik Tok time's up
What will you view?
Will you swipe left
or scroll up to see
More beer, booze,
and self inflicted tragic news
That will fill your
Secular cup?
Yes, you're desensitized
Will it be to late
Before we participate
In voting for
another president
to win a debate
to try to facilitate
a semi normal nation
that only God
Can truly determine our fate
of a fallen world
lukewarm Christianity
we negate
No more morals will
I negotiate
As I fall to my knees
Begging please
Let me enter through
The narrow gate
God heal our world
from this
fucked up state
before it's too late
Feeling entitled
Oozing with pride
I roll my eyes
Jump in my Uber
and disappear
while still scrolling
in my ride
Feeling completely empty inside

Don't Drink the Wrath (My Cup)

[#Poem #Sin #Backslide #DrugUse #Addiction #StrongSexualContent #ExplicitLanguage #Suicide #EndTimes Rated M]

Jezebels, and broken vows
The day of death is near
What fortune tells
is not savory
to this New World Order
In store
for every filthy whore
Forever more
the Devil is tactfully keeping score
While sex sells on every corner
HIV infection causing
mass destructive war
Alongside vaccinated zombies
Trying to avoid COVID
knocking on every door
Black and ice galore
Pills and bottles everywhere
Left you ill, puking everything
But your dignity on the cold hard floor
Yet we continue to fall
Crying out, "my veins need more!"
Death is soon in store
for the deviant behaviors
We seem to adore
This is not what this nation
has fought so hard for
No more insanity
and self inflicted vanity
from a humanity
Thinking we are all that
Lying through and exaggerated IG filter
And sexting through Snapchat
An unliked post hurts the most
When your presence
Appears to be merely a ghost
Do you hear a knock at the door
Candy left by the predator next door
You always seem to avoid

The truth as you believe the lie
This world is nearly over
You cry out
"I just wanna fucking die!"
Why God why do I not try
To see a better life
From You to I?
Rainbow flags of pride
I use to hide
the Man of God inside
Please God
End this reckless ride
I just want to feel love
And stop the hovering
Thundercloud above
Please give me love
I need Your love
Don't ever let me give up
I no longer want to drink
From sins deadly cup

Treading on the Aftermath

[#Poem #Sin #Backslide #DrugUse #Addiction #StrongSexualContent #ExplicitLanguage #Surrender #Freedom Rated M]

Treading on the aftermath
Of the lonely pain left inside
The devil's hit that cycle again
knocked me down
with another boost
of ego, hypocrisy, and selfish pride
hard, and much more deadly
than any hurricane's category 5
Losing all confidence
in the man I once was
My sunken eyes have
Once again hit the floor
The masquerade of lies
Are now over
To no surprise
Soon auntie Tina
Will be knocking at the door
I scream at the mirror
What have you done
you fucking filthy whore?
Tragedy is your middle name
Death is keeping score
You will never be respected
You've inflicted far too much
guilt, and shame
Your life will never be the same
Now die from the pain
and never smile again
Laying on the ground
Nearly given up on all hope
I'm at the end of my rope
I surrender, and swear off of dope
Please come, and save my life
I no longer want to be
a slave to the grave
I no longer want to betray
and misbehave
I watch it all fade away
Yes I burned my dreams

I confess my sins to You
The God of second chances
You've forgiven and forgotten
all that I have put You through
No temptation has authority
to take dominion
over my redemption story
You have picked me up
and call me son
The victory over
death, addiction, and destruction
are done
By Your stripes I am healed
The battle of the fallen man
Has finally won
By the Father, Spirit, and the Son
Treading on the aftermath
This intentional journey
Was not so bad
To grow a grateful heart
I am free from a life
That was wicked and so sad
Chosen to restore the pain
My life will never be the same
Though I may have to hurt again
The shackles of defeat
have finally fallen off my feet
The curse is broken
and FREEDOM has my soul
Still treading on the aftermath
God You will ALWAYS be in
control

Why?

[#Poem #Depression #Suicide #Surrender]

Why does it seem that the one standing next to me is more blessed than I?
Why does it seem that the more I try to repress goodness unto others,
I never seem to see the same reflection?
Why is that I'm always the one to comfort you?
Why does it seem that there is no point in anything that I do?
Why do I cry when there is no one here to care?
I asked myself not why, but how to put an end to this despair?
I'll change my actions, and put a smile on my face
Positivity over a negative attitude will always win the race
No more feeling sorry, as I open up my eyes
Another day, I'm grateful
God's gift has turned out to be such a beautiful surprise!

One Man's Trash (I Am Still...)

[#Poem #Sin #Backslide #DrugUse #Addiction #StrongSexualContent #ExplicitLanguage Rated M]

Write me off for the
deviant wrong doings
that once 'bated' my life...
Jack me off the edge,
as Jezebel continues
to stir up strife,
and perverted lies
to disguise the jaded,
and hated man of God
hidden underneath sin...
Who am I to take
the responsibility
of your guilt, and sometimes
undeserved judgment
for so long?
According to the book
of hypocrites
(an unwritten chapter of the Bible
unfolding day by day)...
Came back to Colorado
too soon
some seem to say...
Sentenced to a life of shame,
rejection, and ongoing cycles
of bitterness and rebellion...
Illusions of hope to get off of dope
fade away like the integrity
I once had...
Well guess what,
God still shines bright
unto my path!
Though you can't see
the aftermath of your
self inflicted tragedies...
Plagued by the rise,
the fall, and surprise demise
come full circle again...
PQ may be a pawn to you

that's easily disposable...
But, God still holds the pen
until the end!
Jesus takes the wheel,
and the Holy Spirit will guide
this prodigal's life once again!
His promises to fill my life,
as I leave behind
your spoken curses
that once had me bound...
I am still called to love…
I am still called to heal…
And, I am still called
to help the hurting world
one soul at a time
starting with myself…
Those that are meant
to stay will stay,
and those who are not will stray…
Take your bets, kick up dust,
or hold your place…
Send me on a plane, I won't stay…
One man's trash,
is another man's treasure...

I can see the sun again!
My Faith sees far beyond
the Rocky Mountains...
Home is where the heart is...
Purpose is being built bigger
than any dollar sign, any drug,
or any pleasure from this day
forward!
That is something that is
souled out for Jesus, and not
for sale to the world...
Spoken against, yet irrevocable…
Manipulated, yet never controlled
by man...
God has the map, God knew the man,
and God knows the plan!

The Best View Comes After the Hardest Climb

[#Poem #Relationship #BreakUp #DrugUse #Rejection #Homosexuality #Redemption #Surrender #Freedom]

Just because I smile
My pain you never see
How did we develop
A toxic relationship
between you, and me?
Ride or die you've always been
the one to pull me through
The oceans and the valleys
But now our connection
has ended
because of you
You led me through the pain
You led me through the rain
You led me through the war
But, you never led me through the
right open door
You led me to the needle
that I put inside my vein
You led me to the wrong lane
Which caused me to go insane
With lies that clouded up my brain
inside my head
was everything that you said
broken promises you made
that now surround me
You made a mess in the bed
you now have to lie in
Good thing for you
I gave up, and stopped crying
No more trying hard
to abandon me
A perfect person
plastic as can be
I have overcome the rejection
you chose not to see
I now seek the One
who is perfectly made for me
I turn away from sin
My life restored
As I give all in for the win

I turn away from pride
The rainbow was never yours
So I close all doors
A new life with Him
I now decide
Taking back the promise
that was lost along the way
No more trauma in my life
Please don't label me as gay
All I want to say
Is how He restored my hope
This mountain that I climb
With faith being my invisible rope
This journey has a goal
I will keep this smile on my face
Through tragedy or victory
No matter what life brings
I WILL finish this race!

One Man Stands Alone

[#Poem #Rejection]

He barely knew how to survive without his daddy's love.
He barely knew how to thrive, while living life knowing her family
was sadly more important.
Not knowing how to stand alone as a man, as one is supposed to.
He secretly weeps, and wishes to one day
capture his daddy's love.

Reign and Righteousness

[#Poem #DrugUse #Addiction #Depression #Encouragement #Recovery #Restoration]

As I close the blinds
to obscure any light
that has plans to shine hope
to this life that I nearly
wrecked with dope
I remember...
there was once a man
full of promise, talent,
and ambition...
Symptoms of success
seem to dilate a life
once displaying 20/20 vision
for a purposeful vessel
created to rescue,
and not execute...
I dissect every word
of encouragement
that has been spoken
over the past quarantine
that has barely
cradled this desolate shell..
Mom's pride, and joy
has nearly crumbled her heart,
Her hopes, and her dreams
to honor her son who is called
by God to carry revival
to the nations...
Will he ever rebound,
and gain momentum
to reign in righteousness?
Only time will tell,
As I fly from the nest
integrity is at test...
Time for recovery, and rest...
Day 2 day I pray to stay...
Mighty, and faithful
God please bless this day!

Coming Out of the Other Side

[#Poem #DrugUse #Addiction #Depression #ExplicitLanguage #Encouragement #Recovery #Restoration]

While you were the lesson
I had to learn
I believed every word
Who would have thought
my heart you would burn
Poison my ears
With fucked up
promises and lies
You never let me see
Past your insensitive disguise
Reality is
I never allowed myself to be
The illusion of selfish love
You always wanted from me
Lovers to friends
The war never ends
I try to fall no more
So I chose to walk out the door
How could you compare me
To the whore you left on the floor
He has no passion
For making happiness last
I could have never given
a better future
Instead I am now a part of your
Purposeless past
Sail away to a different day
When my love for you will fade
You've hurt me One last time
Now I'll be fine
Knowing you'll never be mine
This new life I have made
I would never trade
the sin I felt within
I cut off ties
Don't act surprised
I no longer choose
a sexual experience
With anymore guys
I live my life now

For a celibate ride
And dedicate my love
To a God who will never
Leave my side
I cut ties
Goodbye
The ride is over
Let me go and always know
I cannot love you
So live without me
Let me be free
Sexuality no longer defines
Your hold on me
I am free
Truly free to be me

Grateful 4 (Labels No More)

[#Poem #Relationship #Abuse #Depression #Encouragement #Recovery #Restoration]

Grateful 4 the warmth
that casts away my hesitant why's
Grateful 4 the stars
that illuminates my once clouded over skies
Grateful 4 the tragic
that you try to cover up with superficial lies
Grateful for the the deranged life
I now demise
as your hate always comes as no surprise
Once was a slave
to the shadow you had me hiding in for so long
I learned so much from our distance
Why do I still cry and reminisce
to our jaded and outdated song?
You pulled me along for far too long
hoping that I would finally break

Well guess what… You were wrong!
Because the day I let you win
was my biggest mistake
My heart you have forsaken
by idols and labels you would make of me
To believe I could never be free
from the clutches of a past
I could not throw away too fast
Well I break the chains with faith
In the only One who can wash away my sin
The new identity is in Him
No more labels over my life
I will let you dim
The Holy Ghost I love the most
as the one true guide who's always on my side
He has pointed me to the truth
God's love will never divide

the ordained life I hold with joy and pride
I have finally gotten off the ride
From this day I pray we never meet again
You were never meant for me
Now I see
Labels can never control me
Or define the man of God
I'm truly meant to be!

My prayer is to no longer allow labels define my identity as my love for Him grows stronger!

Finally Found

[#Poem #DrugUse #Addiction #Depression #ExplicitLanguage #Relationships #Encouragement #Recovery #Restoration Rated M]

When I'm looking for a man
to bring me an ounce of hope
You let me down again
so I say fuck it
as I run back to dope
Daddy don't you see
your love has never met me
Why does she get to be
in your world I might never see
Because of who you are
I use to run and hide
Because of who you are
I built up so much pride
Because of who you are
I pushed love for myself aside
Just blowing in the wind
I feel so lost inside
There once was a man named Skip
My heart he loved to rip
My hopeful life I once lost grip

I sip the pain away caused by Skip
Then there was Jay
He always had something hurtful to say
We used and medicated our lives away
Sadly Jay is no longer with us today
Let me tell you about Harry
The man I vowed to marry
His last name I would carry
Until the abuse became too scary
Because of who you are
I use to run and hide
Because of who you are
I built up so much pride
Because of who you are
I pushed love for myself aside
Just blowing in the wind
I felt so lost inside
Then one day I met a man

who longed to show me love
I tried to run away
but He sent a Holy Dove
Afraid to love again
I surrendered
My walls came crashing down
And now I can't imagine
my life without Him around
Because of who You are
I no longer have to hide
Because of who You are
I let go of all the pride
Because of who You are
I found love for myself inside
No longer blowing in the wind
I am grateful for this ride
Not every man is worthy of the love
poured out by me
But still I choose to forgive
because You have forgiven me
I can finally breathe
My inventory released
into the world
I am free!

Pipeline 2 Perfection

[#Poem Addiction #Recovery #Restoration #Rejection #Surrender]

As I pipeline 2 perfection
Meth and alcohol is no longer my infection
Recovery is my new obsession
No longer do I cope with injection
of a drug led on by rejection
Now I look into the mirror and see a new reflection
A clear complexion
of a man grateful for his Savior's resurrection
Promised to give a new life
with everlasting protection
I choose to follow Him over any man
leading a Presidential election
No more labels of political agendas
or false pride connection
This is my confession of my
pipeline 2 perfection

Living my best….
Spoken words by: Patrick Quezada

"Boulevard of Flying Colors (Step 4)"

[#Poem Addiction #Recovery #12steps #Restoration #Rejection #Surrender]

As I come to the end of myself
I realize that creating a plausible
Christ-like Legacy takes a lot of time
effort, and tenacity...
Turning tragedy into triumph
I am now on a boulevard of flying colors
chasing the promises of
Emmanuel (God With Us)...
No longer will I moronically and insanely
fall through the cracks of sober living
while feeding into self-indulgent behaviors...
A well-conditioned spirit
and lifestyle becomes
my newly chosen fate...
When working the 12 steps
you can count on Jesus' footprints
to carry you into a new
and everlasting recovered life...
Once an addict, not always an addict...
I am healed in Jesus name!
As I take a fearless and moral
Spiritual inventory
victory is on the horizon…

Brandon's Hope

[#Poem Addiction #Recovery #12steps #Restoration #Rejection #Surrender]

Lost among society
a boy who had no hope
Reality he had to face
statistics say
he should be dead by dope
Brandon is his name
and all he wants is to be
Free to love himself
Yes free like you and me
The judges know him well
County clerks
and cops the same
He had no friends to trust
and his family shamed his name
Brandon felt so lost
as crime and dope
controlled his life
He tried to take his life
by pills and rope or a knife
Jail cells and treatment plans
His life was out of control
Nothing seemed to work
not even love
from his girlfriend Nicole
Feeding his addiction
wreaking havoc through his veins
Death is coming soon
if Brandon's life remains the same
As God came to see
what's left of Brandon's broken heart
He calls his son to rise
if only Brandon will do his part
Now Brandon has a choice
to show the world
what he can do
So pray for Brandon today
and hope the same
doesn't happen to you
Forget what you heard
sweep his past under the rug
Brandon will be free
and he deserves all our love

Jacob's Love

[#Poem Addiction #Recovery #12steps #Restoration #Rejection #Surrender]

Alone in the world
with no one to hug
Whatever happened
to Jacob's love?
Many lost years
created too many fallen tears
Always angry
many wounds and fears
Where did Jacob go?
He wrestled with his mind
He wrestled with his flesh
He felt so lost inside
Dope is what he knew best
Flowing through his veins
Jacob flies to the sky
God's beloved son
is so lost
and he can't understand why?
As the days turned to years
Jacob nearly lost all hope
The only way to fix it
is with another shot of dope
Crawling in his skin
He's afraid to be alone
Jacob wants to be loved
but no one
is on the other side
of the phone
He rages and he screams
about many wasted dreams
Bruised and broken
as it seems
This is life and all it means
Before Jacob nods out
in shines an ounce of hope
Will Jacob die alone?
God said nope!
Barely breathing
Jacob is picked up off the floor
God has other plans in store

So much more
Yes son, so much more!
As Jacob lost all strength,
he opened up his broken heart
To the one
who loves him most
with a better chance at life
and a fresh new start
Worth more than double rainbows,
gold, and diamonds in the sky
Jacob, you are so loved
never question why
Just accept it and
love yourself inside

Inspired by Jacob at Woodhaven
By: Patrick Quezada

Ready 2 Relive

[#Poem Addiction #Recovery #12steps #Restoration #Rejection #Surrender]

Trust the process
and stay the course
seems so easy to say
Trial and error is the norm
as I work the steps
to conquer addiction today
"Easy does it," and "Just for today"
with positive affirmations
I live to display
To crawl out of a bottle
and about face from dope
I no longer choose
to live this way
As I cut the rope
I surrender my life
to His Higher Power
"To thine own self be true"
I accept the things I cannot change
and humbly change the toxic things
I use to do

With the helmet of salvation
my entangled mind is finally free
From the lies of never being good
enough
I celebrate my recovery
with destiny, hope, and dignity
Blessed as this metamorphosis
is transforming me
into the brand new
Man of God that you see

Standing Together Shoulder 2 Shoulder

[#Poem Addiction #Recovery #12steps #Restoration #Rejection #Surrender]

Underneath the bridge is where we use to be
Many broken addicts with hopeful dreams
Lost at sea
Noah, James, and Jason in the kitchen pouring coffee to start the day
Greg, Donnie, and John collecting cups for a coffee buzz to stay
Kev, Zachary, and Jordan laughing on the side of the room
Tot, and Tyrik ping pong champs
Zero to one then one to two
Aleksander, Ryan, Mark, and Josh getting that meeting on Zoom
McCoy, Cody, and Brandon reading books to praise the Lord in another room
Joshua cutting hair
Michael, James, and Jeremy doing chores
Dylan, Jesse, and Arlen lifting weights
Big muscles they adore
Charles, and Jason ask the RA's if they can sneak a smoke?
Ty making a scene as him and Patrick crack more jokes
As the days fly by so fast
We wonder how long will our sobriety last?
Thank you Gloria, Tim, Sami, Sheri, Freddie, Shay, and Jeremy for the hope you all give
To follow the Big Book with peace and serenity knowing we have purpose and destiny to live
To those I didn't mention please never feel left out
God favors you so much this I promise without a doubt
Our hearts are forever grateful
Thank you #Woodhaven

Remember to Give Yourself a Break

[#Poem #Addiction #Recovery #12steps #Restoration #Rejection #Surrender]

With a shifting of the atmosphere summer days fly by so fast
I look at Sheri's seats and pray for my beloved brothers recovery to last
They inspire me to be better, I see a hero in every single face
In these walls we've bonded forever
These beautiful memories no one can ever replace
Sheri, you have helped me find a new way to love my life
To know that God makes no mistakes even if I may never seek a wife
God is love beyond any label
We don't need to separate our differences today
We share a love for a better life recovered
Please remember life is meant to be lived this way
So with these true words I leave you
Let the world never allow you to lose sight
Please keep a humble heart full of gratitude and grace
I wish you well
Good morning
Good evening and Good night

2 No Longer Cradle the Craziness

[#Poem Addiction #Recovery #12steps #Restoration #Rejection #Surrender]

I no longer
cradle the craziness
As addiction lost the war
This savage walk is finally over
No longer strung out
will you find me
on the bathroom floor
Dig deep into my past
Fueled with nothing but
resentment, regret, and lies
This broken man
is no longer the same
Why do you look so surprised?
Surrendered to my Savior
As I humbly put in the work
4 meetings a week
A gratitude list
and 12 steps proven to work
A year of being clean
On the other side I see
A loving and faithful
Man of God
Ready to help others
become free just like me
No longer bound by chains
The victory is ours at last
Mighty wounded warriors
We are free
Free at last!

–Say What You Mean and Mean What You Say–

[#Poem #OdeToMother #Apology]

Every moment is a challenge when your heart turns to gray
Mama say what you mean and mean what you say
I was once a little boy who could brighten up your day
Mama say what you mean and mean what you say
Through the trials, tears, and laughter your strength and love took my fears away
Mama say what you mean and mean what you say
Your faith in God helps turn me from disaster
Mama please say what you mean and mean what you say
I was not the perfect son or even your favored one,
but I say what I mean and mean what I say
I try to live a holy life and not let addiction have it's way
I'll still say what I mean and mean what I say
I loved you then and I love you now and I'll love you forever
That's why I say what I mean and mean what I say
I'm sorry it took so long to say these words today
I love you and I forgive you
I hope you love your baby boy the same way

Shattered

[#Poem #Rejection #Father]

As days go by of my teenage years
I think of all the hurt and tears of the pain caused by my father
He's hurt me in so many different ways
I can't even begin to count the days of the disappointment and the deceitful ways
my dad has hurt me
I'm a broken child standing in the dark
Wondering what it would be like to have a true father, and not just some tall stark
man who doesn't even acknowledge my own existence
Sometimes I wonder what did I do?
All I wanted was a normal father
Someone who loves me
Someone who I can love
A positive role model in my life
Not a child thrown away for his wife
Someone who actually gives a damn whether his son graduates, or at least pretends
to care
Oh, well what can I say?
You never believed what happened to me that day
Two older step brothers, who taught me more than how to just play
Things that kids should never have to lay
With two of his step brothers that way
All I can do is hope and pray that someday God opens his eyes before it's too late

That I Would Be Perfect

[#Poem #Backslide #Apology]

I don't know what happened between you and me?
We used to be so close as a mother and a son can be
We used to laugh for hours, it's sad how things can change
You've always been my hero now this relationship we have seems very strange
I remember feeling special to introduce you as my best friend
I promise to love you always mom until the very end
I'm sorry I've never been perfect and I never got to see
How proud a loving mother could be just to accept me for me
I know you always say it's "tough love"
that you can only show
I want my hero back and I want our love to grow
I don't know what else to say?
I don't know who else to be?
I can only hope and pray one day mommy says she loves me
Until that day comes, the Lord has promised to me it would
I love you forever mom
Just know that I would be good
even if I'm not perfect

Blood or Water??

[#Poem #Rejection #Father]

Vivid memories of how daddy used to adore me
Now it is his wife, and step kids he is always longing to see
Somehow I seem to wonder, what is thicker blood or water?
God if only I knew what it would take to reclaim my father?

Please Don't Salt the Wound

[#Poem #Apology #Mother)

Like grains of salt to an open sore
I have no longer an ounce of pride
to stay here anymore
My mother has abandoned me,
and kicked me out of the front door
There is nothing left to say except
this ends the war
I'll give you space so you can live
My heart has nothing left to give
Clip my wings and let me go
I'll fly away
So I can grow

Where's Daddy Now?

[#Poem #Rejection #Father]

A spitting image that's what they all say
How can such a cruel person even think
to betray his only son in such a deceitful way?
It's as if I were considered a cat as just a stray
Why did daddy choose to run away?

Don't Forget to Close the Blinds

[#Poem #MotherSon]

The alarm clock sounds at 6 AM
I don't know who or where I am, then it hits me it's Monday morning
Mom is in the bathroom, brushing her hair as I try to figure out what to wear?
Both in a hurry on our separate way as we begin a brand new day
With a twist of her wrist, the blinds are now open
Now we are outside the place in which we call home
When in reality, it's merely a place where we sleep
As I open the gate for my mom to pull out of the garage,
she rolls down the tinted window of her Saturn
Knowing that we won't see each other until the next morning,
she kisses me and says, "don't forget to close the blinds when you get home"
As she drives to work, and I walk to my bus stop, we each shed a tear when we think
of how selfish we've been for not finding the time to spend together as a family
Another day has gone, and still no effort from either side has been accomplished
I walked through the door, I close the blinds, shut my eyes, and sleep

Practice What You Preach

[#Poem #Forgiven #unforgiveness #Anger #Betrayed #ExplicitLanguage Rated M]

I hate that I trusted you
I hate that you lied
I hate that I had so much anger inside
You pretended to be
my trusted friend until the end
A predator cannot help
a shattered heart mend
The vulnerable man
you preyed on in me
A Pastor should not lie
with any excuse or apology
You carry a cross
Hypocrite you're a fake
You raped my good faith
by your f***ed up mistake
So many people believe
that you are a man of God
Instead you're a phony,
a coward, and a heartless fraud
Now crawl back to the crack
and forget you know my name
God have mercy on your soul
As I pray you never attack
another unworthy victim the same
I'm sorry I showed you
the best part of me
You will never be forgotten
for the abuse you made me see
Numbing with the drug
to no longer feel the pain
As I relapsed, replaying that night
over and over again
made me nearly go insane
Now I sit in treatment
as I write this letter to you
I give my anger and resentments
to the only One
who can pull me through
God, help me not hate you

Written as a release of anger I have
held onto for too long….

Forgiven, not forgotten…

Times Up (Tyler Says)

[#Poem #Unforgiveness #StrongSexualContent #ExplicitLanguage #Recovery #Relapse #Offense #DrugUse #SexualAssault Rated M]

Not nearly enough favor
Tik Tok your time has run out
Did you really think you'd survive
On all of this superficial clout?
Only a matter of time
Before you'd fall off the wagon
And walk the fine line
Of the prideful hill you'd climb
Sold out your momma
For sex with a pig
As you smoke another dime
It's only a matter of time
Before you see
your wasted life fly by
While shooting up another rig
The devil raped you
Lost at sea
Murder in the third degree
Death is in store
For this whore you see
Meth briefly got a hold of me
But Tyler's word curse
And bullshit story
Won't get the best of me
God gets the glory
Of my reconstructed story
The man that helped re "LIT" my fire
Threw me, and blew me away
Called me a fruitless creep
As he fell asleep on his
Bitter black lost sheep
He decided not to keep
the once unreachable mess
I digress
Tyler you're the
Insensitive mess
who got me stressed
Who tried to depress
By turning me into
A fucked up mess
Now guess which step I'm on
You're at the top of my list
As I keep inventory
Am I really ready to make amends
With a bullshit guy
Who will never wonder why

I wasted any tears
on this douche of a guy
I let you in to help me heal
Instead you hurt my heart
Unable to feel real
I take what's left of my self worth
As I run away from you
I break any curse you put
My bleeding heart through
Keep running to Jeffrey
You coward
With every lie untrue
God, and the real one's know me
And will never believe you
Now keep my name
out of your mouth
Same goes for your wife
She's only riding on your
Temporary clout
Freedom fill my heart
I don't need a March to see
How much God really loves
The man I'm meant to be
Never good enough for you
But he's hella loved by me
So keep rejecting me
One man's trash
Is another's treasure
I hope I don't hate you forever
Still broken,

Open My Encrypted Heart

[#Poem #BreakUp #Forgiveness]

Somewhere between saving you, and abandoning me
I'm now held accountable for the desolate faded memories,
and self-inflicted darkness that has found its way into my fragmented heart
I once again find myself empty
Believing in the abundant amount of habitual lies, and shallow promises,
I had to do the only thing my aching heart could do,
and about face this relationship and leave
the man I was inexcusably still in love with
As I'm dying inside
The time has come to recover from the masochism,
we were both shamefully guilty of
By doing the unthinkable, after grieving for so many years
I will now forgive you, as I have forgiven myself,
and pulled out from this pit of torment and tears
as I rise, once again, opening up my encrypted heart
This time, not for a man who hurt me,
but for my Lord and Savior Jesus Christ, the Holy Spirit, and my Heavenly Father
that will never leave me nor forsake me

No More (Self Seeking Sanity)

[#Poem #Sin #Addiction #Trauma #Surrender #Freedom Rated M]

Dirty hands are hard to raise
No matter how badly I hurt
I will faithfully continue to praise
Daily dogma trumps
a relationship with the One
Who has forgotten all wrongs
of the pain we caused
and believe cannot be undone
Criminal lives we carnally chase
As we ignore to contribute
goodness to our human race
Speaking of race
Why do we stop running
toward the Master of us all?
As we choose chaos and destruction
Causing one another to stumble and fall
While Vanity Fair seeks to find
Who's the tallest and thinnest models
replicating a plastic and fantastic
Barbie and Ken looking doll?
We ignore to reconcile trauma within
while cutting off loose skin
As we max out our credit cards
seeking material treasures that
will one day rust from the mall
Death by idolizing narcissists
Who don't care about us at all
Turning away from a Heavenly Father
Who sent His only Son
To die on a cross to save a world
who is ungrateful overall
Self seeking sanity is the name of our shame
God heal our land and soften our hearts
Let us realize Christianity is not a game

A true relationship is what You desire
Help us turn away from sin
to avoid eternal death by fire
We could never earn Your heart
I pray to humbly stay close to You
Strive to hear well done my good, and faithful son
Never to doubt Your love
or hear the alternative choice
As you utter from Your lips
I never knew you now depart
Mirror mirror do you see
A grateful man or
A self seeking person within me?
Help me flee from wreaking havoc
and consequence
Let freedom reign and mercy fall
As Jesus Christ's blood is shed
proving His sacrificial love
is our ultimate strength and defense
Now please
Shine Amazing Grace
upon us all!

Finding Purpose Through Your Pain

[#Poem #Addiction #EndTimes #Repentence]

Always looking at yourself for validation
Through polished pride
While deep down your insecurities seem to show
Such a desolate, and destructive side
Posted on a "Fakebook" wall, you climb so high
But your pedestal is bound to crash and fall
As you prostitute your character, you ask
Who is the fairest of them all?
You prey on new fans to brighten up your disillusioned,
And self-centered day
When you should be praying for deliverance for acting in such a
Shameful, and addicted way
When will your reflection become conviction that will project
More than a temporary solution to bandage
The bondage of vain pollution?
Wake up, and realize there is nothing social about the media
That divides us, and desensitizes us
It is however the new revolution led by lies of the enemy,
And sickness by a virus causing mass confusion
Soon leaving a shell of a person barely living
With no hope of a resolution
Protect your peace, and purity
Turn away, and let God propel you into a prosperous future
That He has planned for you today
Show someone true love through actions that need to be

Activated beyond a tweet, a like, a text, and hitting a share button
The enemy wants to destroy us through perversion,
Isolation, masks, and mass destruction
But God will prevail, as we armor up, and take a stand
for truth, and justice
Just put your trust in Him, and turn away from sin

Pandemic

[#Poem #EndTimes]

Don't walk out on the streets
without a mask
Don't breathe!
Put out that cigarette
as your lungs begin to bleed
Why are people in a panic
when we were warned since day one?
Revelation unfolding
we must cling to our Heavenly One
Seeing this Pandemic exterminate
everyone
Without warning, this invisible death
has now begun
God will not be mocked
as He closes down all fun
You can't run, it's too late,
His will, will be done
You can sanitize your hands
all you want, but will it clean
the sin you feel within?
Probably not
Why is it that churches
have to stay closed
yet plenty of dispensaries,
trap houses, and booze stores galore!?
Truly shows what people want more!
Essential activities? I think not...
We must fix our priorities...STAT,
before we get COVID caught!
Greed...Greed you selfish pig!
Don't you know that gluttony is a sin?
You didn't win big by taking so much,
now lonely grandma has to suffer
for lack of all that toilet paper
you hoard that won't even clean up
the mess you made of your miserable life!
Try to be still with the ones you love
Instead of keeping up with the
Kardashians
Quarantine clean means isolation,
and quality time
So disinfect your bitterness
and re-sensitize you're stoney heart
that's been desensitized by a world
of technology as we all fall apart
Let's begin to heal within
Stop continuing to rebel,
and sin by spreading your germs,
and toxic behaviors!
Social distance from things

that wanna take you straight to hell
Grindr, Snapchat, and sexting as well!
Instead love one another
by doing all you can
to stand right before God,
get saved now while you still can!
Be a frontline hero,
not a self centered ZERO!
Truck drivers, nurses,
online teachers...
Amazon, Door Dash,
janitors, and Preachers...
Thanks for all you do,
God has truly blessed our lives with you!
These are the things we took for granted...
Will you run to Him,
or remain abandoned?
God stripped away every idol from today...
NBA playoffs? No way!
Alanis Morissette concert? Not today!
Red carpet premieres, and award shows?
Sorry no!
All because
we chose to idolize man, and money,
over the One
who has now shut down our economy
We are crippled, paralyzed,
and stripped of our PRIDE!
We fall to our faces, cry
exposing our ugly, and self centered side
Why God why?

Oh God , why did we never kept you first?
If I live for You today,
will you save my tomorrow?
I pray...
Until then, I wonder...
Will I ever live to see
my mom proud of me
for beating the addiction
that almost took life from me?
Not only do I gotta beat the drug
I run cycles around,
COVID-19 rises, with body bags
too many to be found!
Surrender your life now,
and don't be counted out!
When He comes on a cloud,
His is the only cloud
I want for my life to inhale
Until then...
Be careful not to touch me,
stay a safe distance away
I'm so sorry I cannot hug you today!

PART 3:
HAUNTED. HUNTED. HEALED.

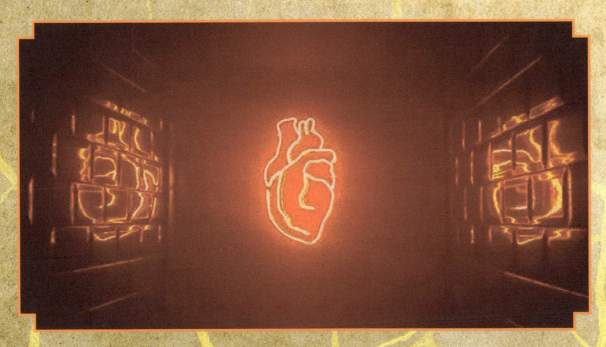

'Create in me a clean heart, O God, and renew a right spirit within me.'
PSALM 51:10

21 Questions

[#Poem #SelfReflection]

If I am grounded, would that make me whole?
If I am altered, would that make you happy?
If I am older, would that make me wise?
I am suffering. Would that one day make me stronger?
I am challenged will I know the answer?
If I am listened to, will I one day be respected?
If I am cultured, will I grow to become optimistic?
I am loved by you will I love you in return?
If I am hated, does that make me a bad person?
I am innocent, will I one day be free?
If I am guilty, will I one day be forgiven for my mistakes?
I am forgiven will you one day let me back in your heart?
If I am overlooked, will I one day be remembered?
If I am wrongfully accused, will you one day feel bad?
If I am encouraged, will I one day succeed?
If I was blind, would you help me see?
If I was cold, would you keep me warm?
If I was hungry, would you give me something to eat?
If I hurt you, would you forgive me?
If I am forgotten does that mean that I wasn't important?
If I died, would anybody miss me?

You Are The (God of...)

[#Poem #Inspirational #God #Faith #Christianity #Tribute]

You are the God of light
in a world full of darkness..
You are the God of freedom
in a world full of entrapment...
You are the God of sovereignty
in a world full of chaos...
You are the God of redemption
in a world full of sinful nature...
You are a God of Integrity
in a world full of deception...
You are the God of recovery
in a world full of addiction...
You are the God of amnesty
in a world full of execution...
You are the God of Blessed Assurance
in a world full of ambivalence...
You are the God of possibilities
in a world full of hopelessness...
You are the God of donation
in a world full of gluttony...
You are the God of restoration
in a world full of destruction...
You are the God of direction
in a world full of confusion...
You are the God of discipline
in a world full of rebellion..
You are the God of celebration
in a world full of grievance...
You are the God of hospitality
in a world full of neglect...
You are the God of endless mercy
in a world full of punishment...
You are the God of no limitations
in a world full of restriction...
You are the God of Amazing Grace
and I am nothing without Your love
and without You in my life...
Surrender to Christ, and not to the world
be the apple of God's eye...
Submit to God, resist the devil, and he will flee!

Born to Save (God With Us)

[#Poem #Inspirational #God #Faith #Christianity #Tribute]

Born to save you and me
His righteousness fulfilled...
A perfect promise
to this malevolent world...
A blameless child
behold we are healed...
Treasures out of darkness
we illuminate the sky...
No longer covered by
darkness and shame
we have newfound purpose
as we are given a chance
to soar and fly high...
Confessing to the world
that You are my hero
was the best decision
I have ever made...
Your book of promises
I hold dear to my heart...
Jesus my love for You
will never fade...
God With Us, I trust You
to always be my light...
I will do my best to be Your salt
giving as much enriched flavor
to the life You have given me...
King Jesus You are my life
You are my love
and You are the foundation
holding this imperfect person
together..

God's love is (God is love)

[#Poem #Inspirational #God #Faith #Christianity #Tribute]

As the leaves start to turn again,
I can tell it's coming the time of the year
to bundle up and be thankful to have one another
To give thanks to Him for blessing us with another safe year ending
This winter and holiday season, I'm going to try something a little bit different, instead of being upset that God has allowed me to be cold and homeless
while grieving what I have not
I will rejoice and celebrate what I will always have, God's love
You don't need to experience God's love at the dinner table
once a year on Christmas Day
His love is all around all year-round
God's love is writing a letter to those who have hurt you in the past
letting them know that you forgive them
God's love is offering your brother the jacket off of your back
when you see that they are shivering with hardly any clothing at all
God's love is complementing somebody for something special
that they bring to your life,
while you made their day, and putting a smile on their face,
instead of criticizing or complaining about them,

and the things that they have not accomplished to fulfill your own selfish desires
God's love is being homeless and incarcerated
and humbly accepting a fellow inmate's piece of bread when hungry,
even though he may not be the same color, background, or sexual orientation
We're all God's children and we all bleed the same
When Jesus died on the cross, His blood was shed so that our sins may be forgiven
Just because I don't exactly have a home right now
doesn't mean that I'm angry with God in anyway
I know that He has great plans in store for my future
I humbly accept any roof over my head, in the meantime
Understanding all around us every day how different people are
is a part of Christian growth as I have learned today
God bless everyone and may you all rejoice this holiday season,
knowing God is love amen.

Days Like This

[#Poem #Inspirational #God #Faith #Christianity #Tribute]

Days like this I want to say
How grateful I am for You
each and every single day
My heart for You
is faithful and true
I trust in You
for all that I continue
to walk through
My life was paid
on the cross You bare
I smile because
You love me so much
when no one else was there
I promise to try to give my all
From this day forward
I hope to never again fall
Please help me stay
forever this way
Days like this
I'm grateful today

Truth Plus Grace Equals Love

[#Poem #Inspirational #God #Faith #Christianity #Tribute]

You can't truly love someone
unless you're willing to
offend them with the truth.
Truth without grace will break you…
Grace without truth won't bless you…
Make sure the light you inspire with isn't really darkness.
If God is for us, it doesn't matter who comes against us…
Truth Plus Grace Equals Love!

Who U R

[#Poem]

By this, all people will know that you are My true disciple… if you have love for one another!

God's Perfect Answer

[#Poem #Inspirational #God #Faith #Christianity #Tribute]

When the world counts you out
and all odds are stacked up against you
Remember that your life's equation
God can only figure out
There isn't a single problem
He can't solve
He loves you one hundred percent
So when you decide to subtract
all of the negativity out of your life
and add a better attitude of gratitude
with a healthy atmosphere
The sum of your life will equal
God's perfect answer

Power 2 Change

[#Poem #Inspirational #God #Faith #Christianity #Tribute]

When sin has shifted the world
and hope doesn't seem
to stand a chance
Faith will lift my eyes
raise my hands
and I will dance
like David danced
They say a vaccine
can take away
the chaos and destruction
we all face today
But that is not the way
The answer is simple
Just lift up your heart
kneel down
and pray to the One
who will never lead you astray
and deliver you from sin today
The time is near
to end all fear
So the choice is yours
to walk with God
and close all other doors
Do not change yourself
to fit the world
Change the world
to follow Jesus

"Dear Addict"

[#Poem #Addiction #DrugUse #Recovery #EatingDisorder #Surrender #Freedom]

When you feel so far gone
and feel like you don't have
a single friend in the world…
Just know that you are forgiven
for the distress you have selfishly
inflicted upon yourself
and the poor victims
who have always loved you
no matter what…

You are not alone in this world
of beautifully broken
compassionate
and talented individuals
suffering from the disease
called addiction…

Addiction is the face
of the single mother
barely surviving day by day
wondering what she has done
to deserve abandonment
from her family…

Addiction is the face
of your over-worked teacher
not knowing another way
to deal with daily stress…

Addiction is the face
of your alcoholic father
you have nearly given up hope on…

Addiction can be the face of you
Addiction was the face of me…

What you choose to do with your life
beyond this realization
is completely up to you…

Will you continue to use?

Excuses after many endless excuses
How many times can God
give you a chance to turn it around?

Depending on a substance
to be a crutch while barely surviving
is not how God has intended
your life to be...

Don't let addiction be the end of you
You are a beautiful bird
who can be set free once and for all...

All you have to do is believe
in yourself as much as the ones
you continue to hurt...

"Point 2 U"

[#Poem #Inspirational #God #Faith #Christianity #Tribute]

Too many tears I've wasted feeling sorry for this man who has had free will to heal a wounded heart from falling apart time after time again, if only he'd surrender...

Too many years I've chosen to walk away from success, and happiness destined for a healthier me that I was created to be...
Instead, choosing to run off to the races...
I fell back into familiar cycles...
Seeing the same ol' faces...
Looking for love in all the wrong places...
I would tiredly continue running around in circles over and over again...

Too many hearts I have broken with selfish ambition, and empty promises...
I embraced vainglorious desires, while looking down upon others...
When I should have been living my life humbly chasing His glory, and falling on my face giving thanks for rescuing and restoring this unworthy, and once addicted man...

Now how grateful one can be, for all You have opened these once blinded eyes to see...
A better life was meant for me, as I focus on helping others to be set free from chains, and bondages not meant for them or me...

Yes we are free... Finally free!

If only we remain obedient, and fall upon our knees to please You, and not man...

Thank You Heavenly Father for all You do...
I am forever grateful, that's why I point to You!

"Mighty Men of Valor"

[#Poem #Inspirational #God #Faith #Christianity #Tribute #Recovery]

Through God all things are possible
for He saved you and me
Blemished sinners of this world
unlock our shackles
we are finally free
Alcoholics, and dope fiends
together we unite
By the grace of God
we are saved
So put on your armor
and prepare to fight
Misfits to the world
we no longer rip and roar
A new life we begin
As God has promised us
so much more
Mighty Men of Valor
the Holy One we must revere
For in God we must always trust
as the devil has no authority
to control our fear...

"U Were There (I Surrender Once And For All)"

[#Poem #Inspirational #God #Faith #Christianity #Tribute]

U were there to encourage, and favor me (Your beloved), when I soared high above the appointed, and anointed rest while proving my loyalty, and obedience to You at the beginning, and end of everyday...

U were there to be faithful, and patient to me even when I wasn't at my best to pass even the simplest empathetic, and apathetic test failing time after time again only caring about myself as I smile, and snap another selfie to post on my superficial Fakebook wall of shame...

U were there to see me rise above this tempted and sinful flesh as I'd pick up my cross, and die to myself everyday to prove my love to You by no longer idolizing materialistic goals, violent and masochistic roles, and perverted souls who want to do lustful things to me provoking me, and trying to take me straight to hell...

U were there to forgive this once addicted and self-centered psychopathic mess who would show nothing but self inflicting actions while pushing away everyone, and anyone who tried to show me how to be loved through a "normal life"...

U were there to see me rise above it all...
U were there to witness my prideful, and shameful fall...

U were there when I built up a wall of lies to disguise the coward I was trying to hide inside through shooting meth into my veins to numb the pain of barely existing...

U were there when I finally heard Your voice, and answered the call...

U were there when I surrendered my life once and for all...

No longer controlled by my emotions, I focus on the bigger picture...
His purpose, not my plans...
I believe in true love again...
I am forgiven, so I can forgive myself...
No longer held captive, I am set free...
These chains are broken once and for all…
I surrender!

"Beauty From Ashes (Phoenix Rising)"

[#Poem #Inspirational #God #Faith #Christianity #Tribute]

How can I forget
the day you saved me?
Yet, how can I relent the way
the world betrayed me?
You've made beauty from these ashes
of my frigid, and broken heart...
I now sing praises to the Lord
for my furbished
and reconstructed new start...
I will rise to the top
as I bury generational curses
with blessings of obedience...
I am promised to be the head
and not the tail...
I will be set on high above
all the nations on earth...
Blessed in the city
and blessed in the country...
Blessed when I come in
and blessed when I go out...
The Lord will grant that my enemies
who rise up against me
to be defeated before me...
They will come at me from one
direction
yet flee from me in seven...
The Lord will bless everything
I put my hands too as long as
I keep true in all I do for Him...
I will lend to many
yet borrow from none...
Blessed are the pure in heart
for they will see God...
Blessed are the peacemakers
for they will be sons of God...
And blessed are those
who are persecuted for righteousness
for theirs is the Kingdom of Heaven...
Amen!

Finding a New Normal

[#Poem #Addiction #Inspirational #God #Faith #Christianity #Tribute]

Showing nothing but wasted talent
so many years have gone by…
Time passes, and I wonder why
I continue to drink, and get high
to numb the pain I feel inside?
As my tears hit the pavement
I sink to a new low…
Welcome to reality
when guilt, and shame is all I know…
As I live my life in chaos
I continue to cope with booze, and dope
Falling from sanity is normal
while beginning to lose all hope…
Crawling on my face
once labeled as a fiend
Until God loved me off the streets
now I'm grateful to be clean!

"Maybe Today"

[#Poem #Inspirational #God #Faith #Christianity #Hope #Restoration #Tribute]

Maybe today
will be different...
Maybe today
I will smile, and not be sad...
Maybe today
you will love me...
Maybe today
I will love myself...
Maybe today
I won't feel like a burden...
Maybe today
I won't be judged for my past...
Maybe today
I won't fall back into addiction....
Maybe today
I will be the one being served for once...
Maybe today
I'll be accepted and not made fun of...
Maybe today
I'll be picked first instead of last...
Maybe today
I can openly praise, and worship God
the way I know how without being
called a distraction...
Maybe today
I can trust you…
Maybe today
I won't want to leave...
Maybe today
I will truly feel part of a family...
Maybe today
I won't feel like the only child...
Maybe today
I need a hug...
Maybe today
I'm the one who needs encouraging...
Maybe today
will be better than yesterday...
Maybe today
I can forgive you...
Maybe today
I can be forgiven...
Maybe today
I can finally, and firmly be planted…
Maybe today
I can grow…
Maybe today

In the Shadow of Your Wings

[#Poem #Inspirational #God #Faith #Christianity #Tribute]

I look to You once more...
Isn't it ironic that I'm here once again?
Here in an empty museum of my just desserts...
My aching eyes close, and my tired fists turn to open hands
I'd like to say that I've taken every hit, and stood in every battle...
Yet, that's not true...
I've laid down, and slept...
Played to quit on purpose...
Yet, it's You...
And only You...
You've been my rock...
You've been my rescue...
You enabled me to stand...
Up again!
And now, I decide...
I'll raise these hands
I'll praise Your name once again!
Let my ways be Your ways...
I give my heart to You...
As I let You piece it back together from a point others call, "no return"...

Lord, here I am again...
Breathe life anew
Into my hopelessness...
A diamond in the rough longing to shine...
Remember, every beautiful sparkle has to first endure much pressure...
They say that at the end of every rainbow is a pot of gold...
That myth is too tired, and too old to be told...
Truth is...
The rainbow's beauty lies in its promise from God to stop the extinction of our very own existence...
Drowning from destruction brought on by selfishness, and rebellion...
The rainbow is also a badge of honor, and a symbol of victory for the storms we have faithfully endured!

Written by: Patrick Quezada & Victor Franco

'Love's Journey to Surrender'

[#Poem #Inspirational #God #Faith #Christianity #Freedom #Restoration #Tribute]

As I tremble towards surrender
Desperate for healing
I find grace I could never earn
I let go of the biggest stumbling block
myself
More than anything
I need Your love to cover my scars
Is it true that even I can be forgiven?
A whisper beyond the mirror
Says 'Look at the beauty of what I've
created.'
Desperate for acceptance
I find mercy in my weakness
I let go of things of my own creation
More than anything
I need Your kindness to help me love
again
Is it true that even I can become
whole?
Memories of thunderclouds
have finally dissipated
Brighter days are surely ahead
More than anything
I need Your strength to keep moving
forward
no matter how hard things might get
Is it true that even I can find purpose
to live a prosperous life?
Gifts, and tokens of a past life
speak from their silent resting place
The past waves, weakly fading
I need Your light
to see the cloudless sun
Is it true I too am guarded by angels?
Wanting to open my heart to trust
again
Spoken words have fallen flat
Will it be different this time if I
believe?
I need Your guidance to discern reality
Is it true that even I can learn the
difference

between what is fact
and what is fiction?
Desirous to apprehend a light that calls
It outshines my preconceived beliefs
Calling me to a new level of submission
Can I thrive in unknown waters?
I need You to place in me Your desires
Is it true that You seek to entrust
with something new?
No longer chasing fantasies,
bad behaviors, and toxic tendencies
This new fire burns brighter than ever
before
I need Your Spirit to lead me
now more than ever
Is it true that I can be trusted
to help lead others to find salvation?
You beckon me closer
Drawing me in, saying 'embrace My
crucible, embrace My love'
I shudder, falling to my knees
In hope of all You've promised me
Is it true that You would use me to
reveal
something formerly unseen?"
As I open my eyes
I awaken this heart of flesh
that was once stone cold
It's a new day
As I hold onto Your promises
Yes it is true I am renewed
from the former things that use to
sting
Dead to desperation
I finally unpack resentful baggage
that once weighed me down
A new me
Free as can be
So begins
Love's Journey to Surrender

Time Will Tell

[#Poem #Romance]

As the snow begins to pile a mile high, so does the amount of love I feel for you. Though the streets are frozen, and empty, my heart is finally starting to thaw out. Trust is becoming an action beyond words I thought were a fairytale. Before we move too quickly, we must spiritually fast to hear from the One who has the answer at last. Until then, I will embrace you as more than just my friend. Will you be my happily ever after? Time will tell in the end.

"Cut From the Same Cloth" (Poem for Victor)

[#Poem #Romance]

Knit to the the soul
My loneliness no longer takes toll
You have come into my life
Like a breath of fresh air
A covenant with you
My beloved I promise
to always be there
Brothers in Christ for life
The other half of a heart
not broken anymore
You have picked up the pieces
and stitched them together with love
The missing piece to life's puzzle
has been found
It was you all along
Together we stand against naysayers
who may think that our relationship is wrong
But who are they to say
My love for you is not labeled as gay
If David can love Jonathan
I can hold you close

When you have a bad day
that's when I promise to show you love most
Thank you for showing me
that I can finally see
Worthy of true love
As we are meant to be
Free to soar among the stars
You're my favorite
I'll forever cherish this love of ours
The greatest part is
God's hand is the third strand
As long as we keep Him first
This love will fall into His plan
Hold on tight, we're in for a ride
This journey walking with you
Gratefully by your side

Yours sincerely devoted,

-Patrick Quezada

Fallen Out of Sync

[#Poem #BreakUp #Deliverance #Freedom #Surrender]

If I could see You face to face
To dwell in Your presence
To inquire personally
I would ask You quell
The rising tide of dreams and
questions…
Meanwhile…
So often more than not
I would try to climb so high
to reach a destiny called utopia
When deliverance
should have been my focal point…
I seize the moment and reflect
How demons and angels
would wrestle
Who will win this tug a war?
If I could grasp Your garment's hem
To know depths of Your mysteries
To see whispers of Your glory
I would praise You
Embracing Your deliverance and
healing arms…
To make the blind eyes see
Yet why won't You perform
this miracle for me?
I don't deserve this kind of love
Still You peruse me
so I raise my hands
singing hallelujah
To worship You I live…
Forever grateful for
the healing
that is yet to come
I hold onto faith
as I pray without ceasing…
If I had the strength to endure
I would dream and not faint
Although I'm not perfect
Still I will stand without wavering
On what You've promised me
Your unconditional love
Surrounds me as a shroud
I receive, praising You for hearing
You who hear, You who listen
Let this be my love's song
A sweet melody meant for You
As I harmonize in sync
It is Your anthem that captivates

this new relationship that I cherish
Worship is more than just a song
It is the purpose of which
You have created me for
As I live to honor You
I fall upon Your feet
Majesty I am forever Yours
Beyond fantasy, my own reality
I declare I'm Yours to cherish
I have always been Your vessel
As Your chosen clay, I cry
'Potter, direct my steps…
Your will is what I long to fulfill…
Walk me into divine purpose…
As only You know how to do'
Unchanging, all-encompassing
Beyond time, my own perception
Rules Your love upon me
It is a blazing iron, searing
What I must know beyond knowing
Your love will cover
The sea of regret I was drowning in
No longer damaging to my soul
At last…It has drained, and dried up
Like Jericho walls
The past that would haunt me
for so long
is finally starting to crumble
and fall to the ground
I wave my white flag
No longer hiding, as I stand
I muster up enough courage
to fight for my rights and
freely love like never before
This romance starts to bloom
Overshadowing former
gloom, and doom
I partner in Your presence
Forgiven not forgotten
We breathe new life
Conforming not to the patterns
of this world
but to the algorithm of eternal bliss
Your kiss has unlocked my
Once encrypted heart
I live for You
To die is gain
I say, I attest
Yes, it is true to die is blessed
'Come closer,' You bid me gently
I shudder at the thought
Of such a great love
Of such a great price paid
For me, a lover without a true face
A face that transformed
No resolution or shape

With every soul passing
Their look burning judgment
Aching, I yearned to be set as flint
Deep inside I cried in agony
Heard the echoes of a heart resolute
Yearning above all to please You
As I return to the narrow path
I undoubtedly choose to forfeit
this deadly cup of wrath
If only Eve had obeyed God's
command
Before indulging in sin
from a bite that would cancel
everything that was right
This tug of war would be no more
Demons and angels
would no longer have to keep score
The rebellion teetering
that has infected
the world we will continue to witness
fail us time and time again
Until the day of judgement
when the trumpet sounds
The sky will crack open
Riding on a cloud
will be the reverent One
who is mighty to save
More than a million miracles

I embrace this new name
You have so faithfully given me..
I now know
You are never too far…
Forever I'd wait for this One
Author of the beginning
Harbinger of the end
Yes, He's reclaimed a heart
Once thought too far gone
Frozen in its bitterness
Paralyzed by its mistakes
Rotting in its guilt
Doomed to cope alone
Without Him stewing, waiting
Yet, He's met my heart
Beset it with grace and mercy
Entrusted it to one with care
Dare I trust the hands
Whom He gave it to?
Dare I step into the unknown
To walk in fullness of His joy?
Though I've fallen more than seven
My love for You will never
keep me locked out of Heaven
It's true that trust is a fine line
between the past and the future
I choose to lay my life on the line
for the one my Father has

encouraged me to hold onto
As I cut the cord of malice
Solace is my favorite new aroma
Finally home at last
We both let go of our crippling past
As I take hold of your hand
I understand
Never to break your heart
Pure bliss behind your kiss
Your wish is my command
This love of ours has grown so fast
Will it last?
Time will tell…
Only if we let go of our abominable past…
Tears of joy we cry at last!
As the light comes shining through
I open the shutters
Wiping the unfruitful haze from my eyes
I realize you were merely a dream
Happy forever we did once seem
We have forever fallen out of sync

Written by: Patrick Quezada & Victor Franco

Deliver Me From Myself

[#Poem #Relapse #Recovery #Deliverance #Restoration]

How could he be afraid of the rain, when he's ALWAYS been the perfect storm?

Judge me for my past, I'll say I don't regret...Too many times I have sat alone with only myself to who has posed an eternal threat...

The enemy has only so much to blame, for the tragedy I always face when addiction is the same tangled in the game...

Jesus come into my heart once again, and help me humbly see... That freedom is within reach, if I surrender my will to Thee...

From this day forward, let my self-hate come to rest... As I carry my cross, and put righteousness on my chest

With a call that's irrevocable, I get up from a fall...Dead to the sinful man I was never meant to be...

Part the sea, let me see the man of God I'm truly meant to be...

Reignite the fire within me, burned are the bridges to those who are not meant to surround me...

Time to march again, as I faithfully walk into destiny

Resiliently yours forever,

QP

Brave 2 Be Broken

[#Poem #Inspirational #God #Faith #Christianity #Healing #Hope #Restoration]

(A Letter of Hope to my Younger Self)

Tired of hurting, and haunting your past
with lies that blanket you today
God sent me to bring you hope in knowing that
you don't have to live life this way
Dear younger me,
I know why you feel so sad
Neglected and rejected by your alcoholic dad
Not the popular one in school
It isn't your fault that kids can be so cruel
With a mom who wanted perfection
with no flaws that the eye can see
Instead, you chose to be gay
letting the rainbow define you and me
I'm here to encourage you to be strong
and stand still
You will get up the hill
to overcome the drugs that nearly had you killed
The truth is you are loved more than anyone who labeled you a mistake

Patrick, please forgive yourself
What's it gonna take?
God is so proud of you
and wants to pull you through
The mountain of depression
that lives inside of you
Be free, and true to you
I love you
No one can live your life, but you
Talented, courageous,
Compassionate, and strong
You are all of this and more
Chin up Man of God
keep moving forward
Shut the door on your past
Forgive yourself
Surrender your pain and begin to soar
into the life that God has in store

Freedom Means 2 Me

[#Poem #Inspirational #God #Faith #Christianity #Healing #Hope #Restoration]

As I wake up in the morning
To grateful not to see
The beautiful life I now live
Even through this fallen world
full of heartache and tragedy
Just because I smile
Doesn't mean I never cry
The difference is today
I choose to live
and not to die
I surrender my heart
To the One who will
give me a better life to live
As I sparkle like a diamond
in the sky
Frozen bitter words
No longer have need to fly
I will fill up my space
With a positive replace
From the bitterness and lies
Gravity pulls me down
From a once prideful place
I was so lost in space
Now I'm brave enough to see

What freedom means 2 me
another day without substance
To numb the pain within me
You see me for who I am
No longer chained to your feet
What freedom means 2 me
No longer lost at sea
Let me be me
That's all I want to be
Freedom means 2 me
Finally loved by me
The one who
Locked up my heart
And threw away the key
Happiness is my destiny
A normal life you now see
Forgiven and driven
That's what
Freedom means 2 me

This I Promise You

[#Poem #Inspirational #God #Faith #Christianity #Tribute #ExplicitLanguage]

Today's a new day
The clouds have finally cleared
The fallen life I once lived
Is now in the rear view mirror
Russian roulette
Many bets were made
If the sexual addiction
And drug abuse would ever fade
The unstable house of cards I built
would never subside my broken life
I would hide, run, and cry
To my neck I would hold
this trembling knife
A slave to sin
Promiscuity would win
Meth, and anorexia
made me look way too thin
Finally a simple prayer
of surrender would begin
My once encrypted heart
I promise to no longer lust over men
This new journey I am grateful to start
I now lay down my life for You
The only One who forgave me
for the deviant sh*t I use to do
I promise to hold on
No matter how hard life gets
I promise to love You unconditionally
Letting go of all regrets
I might never be
The perfect son You deserve to see
But I promise from this day
To stay, and crucify the flesh
That once was killing me
I'm grateful for this new life
Who would have thought
You would one day
give me the desire
To have a wife
A grateful man of God
You raised within me
I promise to see
the greatest gift
is finally learning to love me!

More Than A Dreamer

[#Poem #Inspirational #God #Faith #Christianity #Tribute]

Look into my zealous eyes
and tell me what you see...
A shattered past
of havoc wreaked
or a surrendered life
overdue to be set free?
More than a dreamer
I'm a believer
in the purpose driven
behind my new life...
Called to the task of
saving the hurting people
of this world
the victory is already won
as I reach out to love
the unloveable
move mountains
far beyond the imagination
and shine where
there was once no light...
Because He loved
I can trust...
Because He forgave
I can believe...
Because He saved me
I can overcome...
Because He delivered me from sin
I can have faith in all things possible...
Because He died
I can live...
And because I pray
He will never let me down...

Humble Pie

[#Poem #Inspirational #God #Faith #Christianity #BetterLiving #Goals]

The following affirmation contains eight easy steps for a happier, and healthier living experience.

Step One: Cry when you need to. Know that it is okay to show your true feelings in any circumstance.

Step Two: Never make excuses for something you have done to dishonor your word. Follow through with every promise you make.

Step Three: When you think you're being too hard on yourself, ask yourself the question, "Doth I Protest too Much?" Answer is, never! The more you stand up for what's right, the better the final outcome.

Step Four: Don't take on more than you can handle. Tell yourself, it's not all of me whom is expected to do everything all of the time.

Step Five: When you are aware that there is so-called chaos in a good friend's life, do the best that you can to encourage them while listening for clues that they may be asking for your help.

Step Six: Spend more time with children, while educating them. Be their hero and positive role model. For example, take an hour out of your time to read a to young girl her favorite story book.

Step Seven: When having a disagreement with your partner, do your best to admit your wrongs, and forgive their mistakes. Know that if you continue to hold on to this grudge, you might miss out on the greatest love of your life.

Finally, Step Eight: Cherish everything in life. God has plans to bless you when obediently doing His works. You can expect Him to fulfill your heart's desires. No matter what, pray daily, seek His guidance, and portray yourself as God's greatest trophy, as the rest of the haters eat a slice of humble pie.

Sweet Friend of Mine

[#Poem #Friendship #Tribute #Love #InMemoryOf #RestInPeace]

As the flowers start to bloom,
April fades into June I will always remember
sweet friend of mine
As I feel a soft breeze, I think of all the memories
no one can ever replace
sweet friend of mine
Whenever I needed a helping hand,
he was always there to give the best advice whenever he can
Thank you so much
sweet friend of mine
Whenever I needed to shout and cry
He was always there by my side
Holding me tight, making sure everything was all right
You're my inspiration
sweet friend of mine
In your eyes I always knew,
that the friendship we had was so genuine and true
I will never forget sweet friend of mine
So now it is time to say goodbye
until we meet again within the heavens sky
I love you, my guardian angel
You will forever be
sweet friend of mine

In loving memory of Henry "Enrique" Dorado †

Guardian Angel in the Sky

[#Poem #Friendship #Tribute #Love #InMemoryOf #RestInPeace]

It's been so many years
since my David went away
So many beautiful memories
remembering my best friend everyday
His smile would melt your heart
In such a loving way
My David had to go
So sad he couldn't stay
Dancing in the sky
My David flies so high
Until we meet again
Happy Birthday
To my favorite guy
My brother David
Guardian angel in the sky…

Written with love for my "Punky" David Helding †

Best friends forever, love always,
"Bam Bam" Patrick Quezada

Mikey Strong

[#Poem #Friendship #Tribute #Love #InMemoryOf #RestInPeace]

Mikey is no longer in pain
Freedom was his gain
Deliverance from evil
His life made Heaven's
Hall of Fame
Seated in the presence
of the One who
heals all shame
Mikey graced our lives
with such a selfless name
Waving a banner of hope
We are left to cope
without our beloved
here on this earth
As we carry his legacy
Mighty man of valor
You have Finished the race
Your memory we lift up
with honorable grace
Until we meet again
my friend until the end

In Memory of Michael Martinez †

"Walk With Me This Way" (Jesus said)

[#Poem #Tribute #Grandmother #Love #InMemoryOf #RestInPeace]

Today we come together,
to celebrate this day...
That my grandma
became and angel
Jesus said,
*Walk with Me this way"...
With her eyes fixed on Heaven,
She taught me many things...
I proudly stand before You,
Because she taught me
not to quit,
No matter what life brings..
As we honor her for her love,
We know that this is not the end..
Until we meet again...
No longer an enemy of this world,
I choose to be Jesus' friend...
As my grandma's smile
prepares a path
leading to eternal's beginning,
following a bittersweet end...

In loving memory of Mabel Quezada †

The Heart of the House

[#Poem #Tribute #Grandmother #Love #InMemoryOf #RestInPeace]

The merry-go-round spins as we all kick off our shoes
Grandma's sitting on her porch reading her Sunday morning news
With a twinkle in her eye, she makes her way to the living room,
ready to prepare dinner for the company she is expecting soon
It's nearly a quarter till four when all of a sudden
there is a knock at the front door
Family and friends gather around
Throughout the house, there isn't a single frown
Always to bring a smile to your day,
my grandma lightens the room in such a very heartfelt way
She is the heart of the house

In memory of Beatrice Wanczyk †

Under Construction

[#Poem #Restoration #SelfLove #Overcome #Surrender #Recovery #God #Love #Grace]

They all smile, not knowing the pain I feel within,
so I smile right along with them
To show your feelings makes you a weak link in the chain,
and burden to others
Not feeling so confident,
I try pulling through another day masking over
the empty shell of vulnerability I have become
I will continue to lift you up making sure you're alright,
and taken care of while feeling loved, as I feel nothing
As I head out the door to face another day of loneliness feeling lost
I take a deep breath, put on my sunglasses to hide the tears I wipe away
so you cannot see my honest eyes as I play the part of having it all together
Just because I take a lot of selfies, doesn't mean I have high self esteem
In fact, it's quite the opposite
I do it because I am seeking acceptance, validation, and attention from others
because I have never felt beautiful
God has promised me this emptiness will not last forever,
as I remain faithful to His word
I am tired of being on the fence serving two masters
Breakdown, or breakthrough God is showing through and through

who is the true you?
Somethings gotta give
No more can I depend on substances to numb the pain
of my broken heart, and my broken life
Lithium and meth are no longer the answer to control,
and numb my feelings and emotions
God is the answer!
I fully surrender myself to Him knowing He will clean me up,
and show me the unconditional love I have always been longing for
No more will I feel sorry for myself, and the situations I have put myself in
No more lies, I am tired of fooling the ones I love
while telling them what they want to hear
I am not okay, but I will be soon
Jeremiah 29:11, and Psalm 37:4 promises me there is hope,
and I will never stop believing!
God has given me the power to defeat depression, and I will prevail!
I am powerful, I am compassionate, I am empathetic, I am strong, I am loved, I am invincible, I am confident, I am ambitious, I am courageous, I am determined, I am humble, I am faithful, I am driven, I am passionate, I am valuable, I am unstoppable!

Written by: Patrick Quezada and Rosemarie Quezada

Rescued Not Arrested

[#Poem #Restoration #SelfLove #Overcome #Surrender #Recovery #God #Love #Grace]

Doorway to peace, or a pathway leading to destruction?
Daily devotion to the enemy, or reverence to the Holy One?
A prideful and polygamist heart, or an overflowing gratitude from the prodigal (son?) who not so long ago had fallen temporarily off course?

The choice is mine to spring up a well…Is it water that's refreshing, and full of life, or drawn from a place of destruction, and pollution forever flowing with the stench of sin that is corroded by chaos? Drenched in doubt and confusion, I'm still holding on (this time sober)…

Why is it so hard to achieve trust, and a full surrender? Once faded by substance, and clouded by "mocked religion," God knows I truly have been trying my hardest… Somehow, when offense, leads to defense plans change again… Same destination, different path…Am I standing on quicksand, a landmine, or a miracle? Recovery, or reckoning? Resilient, or reluctant?

Questions not quenched yet, but Your plans, and timing are perfect…I obey, and stand strong in Your presence…It's being still, and not running that I still struggle with…As I surrender my will, and begin to heal…I know that it is Thy will to fulfill…This new season might not have turned out the way the "world" had hoped for, but I know that You're in control, and still cheering me on! Abba, we're in this together forever...If no one else stays with us, I trust that it'll be okay...Either way I still have a reason to praise, because I continue to walk with You through the valley, and climb the mountain top....

"Have I not commanded you? Be strong and courageous. Do not be afraid; do not be discouraged, for the LORD, your God, will be with you wherever you go."
Joshua 1:9

Update... still clean, and sober recovery is going well but would appreciate all the prayers I can get. God knows just pray!

XO, PQ

He Left the 99 (Rescue Me)

[#Poem #Restoration #SelfLove #Overcome #Surrender #Recovery #God #Love #Grace]

Finally, can You see how truly grateful I can be…
You have given me hope in knowing that I don't have to be perfect
in order for You to love me…
Time after time I've been the cause of my own destiny…
Sadly, I wasn't following the directions that You have given…
Running in circles, I have carelessly tried to make a living
by using my own strength and understanding…
I can only imagine how much time I spent on things that never mattered…
I open my heart to You, asking for clarity…
Will I ever be able to understand Your plans fully?
If not, I promise to still faithfully trust You to lead the way every step I take…

Your will be done I pray, Your son I stay

"You're Invited" (Welcome Home)

[#Poem #Tribute #God #Love #Goals]

Hear my cry oh Sovereign Lord,
Your will I want to please...
I open up my wounded heart,
and fall upon my knees...
My tainted hands
I lift to You...
Remove the shame, and pride...
The price You paid upon the cross
In Your wings I will abide...
I hear Your voice,
as You call my name...
Come walk with me my son...
For you have given up the world…
Well done my faithful one...
As I open the gates, and let you in...
you're finally home I say...
To greet my son with open arms...
I've waited for this day...

Written By: Patrick Quezada & The Holy Spirit

PS

[#Poem]

Did I mention how much I love to write poetry?

Basic Instructions Before Leaving Earth

[#Poem #Tribute #God #Love #Goals]

When the time has come, and all is said and done
When you feel like there is no one around to care
When all seems to be lost, and you feel like giving up all hope
Just know that you can find comfort in Jesus,
His love and compassion will never fail you
His power can and will pull you through any situation
His promise will see you through any trial and tribulation
All things are possible through the blood of our Savior Jesus Christ
Doesn't matter what color you are, or what your criminal history is like
His background check is the only one you can be guaranteed to pass
As long as you confess your sins with your mouth, and truly believe in your heart, that Jesus died on the cross, so that sin may be forgiven
Doesn't matter what kind of medication is out there
He is the true Healer, and the One who will set you free from bondage, depression, anger, and anxiety, when giving Him the chance
Stop living in the past with sadness, and regret weighing you down
Accept the Lord in your heart, and receive
A new life
A changed life
A victorious life

Simply pray

Dear Heavenly Father, I am sorry for my sins, and I ask You from the bottom of my heart for Your forgiveness.
I know, and truly believe that Your Son Jesus Christ suffered, died on the cross, was buried, and rose again, so that my sins may be forgiven.
Holy Spirit live in my heart, and guide me daily to obey the God's Word, and works by doing what's right.
All this I pray in the precious and mighty name of Jesus Christ.
Amen.
Now that you have been blessed with the greatest gift ever He's promised eternal life, share it with others!
Forgive those who persecute you by truly allowing yourself to love and pray for their broken hearts, and hurting spirits.
Finally become a vessel for God's army, by leading those who don't know the Lord to the truth of His word through the same simple prayer, while saving souls and walking in the fruit of the Spirit!
Love, joy, peace, patience, gentleness, kindness, self-control, and long suffering

Someday

[#Poem]

Sad to believe
that I may be frozen
How do I see
words left unspoken?
Tell me that I
am not just another
Bridge that you burned
Nothing left to discover
How many times
have I tried
to make you see
That someday you'd want
to love someone like me?
Heart once again
you had
within your grip
Lies and broken promises
you've caused to re-encrypt
Justify your actions
by pushing me away
Will I ever be the one
to capture your love
Someday?

Looking for the Brightside (Absolutely)

[#Poem]

Hidden in Your wings
is where You keep me safe
Not knowing the whole story
These cycles need to break
If I had one wish
I would hold my head up high
Love me once again
before God opens up the sky
Do I try too hard to make you see
the real me?
Absolutely
Do I try to grow up without making
the same mistakes?
Absolutely
Do I pretend to not know the truth
of this game called recovery, drugs,
and solitaire?
Absolutely
This mental war you play to win
While God picks me up off the floor
once more
But then again who's keeping score?

The government plotted
whistleblowers
Demon clones, phones, and stalkers
who initiate this gang war
Retaliate or Redemption?
Surrender goes both ways
Google mania, and Metaverse
Can't even predict these last days
Predator I am not
Your lies won't take you far
A prophet I've become
As God continues to close your
wicked doors
Do I get angry at this fallen human
race?
Absolutely
Do I forgive and love you anyway?
Absolutely
Will I turn away from your selfish
gain
by duplicating my face?
Absolutely

Will I let you commit more crimes
using my social network
and man-made identity?
Absolutely
Will God still protect me and bless me
in front of your puzzled face
and lack of respect to our human race?
Absolutely
You might hold the blueprint
but God holds the pen
So let's continue to coexist
in a world that's bound to end
Let's pretend
Guess what I know my destiny
Do you know yours?
Absolutely
So why clown around and continue
to bring God's plans round and round
Before it's over I pray that
the lost be found
Absolutely

214

PART 4:
PULLING ON HEARTSTRINGS & OTHER THINGS

'Delight yourself in the Lord,
and he will give you the desires of your heart.'

PSALM 37:4

Seventh Step Prayer

[#Prayer #Recovery #Restoration #12steps #Love]

Heavenly Father, I thank You Lord God for who You are, and for what You're doing in my life…I lift up not just a portion of my life, but my whole heart to You…I know that You have made me who I am, a mighty and fearless man of God…You have called, and chosen me to endure the pain, trials, and suffering that I've gone through to be turned around reflecting a beautiful testimony of Your AMAZING GRACE…I pray for the full armor of God…the helmet of salvation to protect my mind, and thoughts against fiery darts of the enemy…

To control my feelings, and emotions…the breast plate of righteousness, to stand righteously and choose that narrow path to walk down with You leading into victory! I pray for the shield of faith, to grow my faith bigger than my fears, and circumstances…the sandals of peace, the gospel of peace that surpasses all understanding…the belt of truth, to never manipulate, or lie to get out of any situation You have not called me to walk…Instead, to be a man of integrity, and good character, showing honesty…and above all else, the sword of the spirit trusting in your Word always and forever to never come back void, to stand on and never be ashamed to share with others!

Please engrave it upon the tablet of my heart, as I choose to walk in the fruit of Your spirit with love, Joy, peace, patience, gentleness, kindness, self-control, and long-suffering…as crucify my flesh, to pick up my cross daily, to follow You and to not look back…I know that in testing of patience will develop into perseverance, and strength if I faint not! I thank you Lord God for allowing me to finally forgive myself for the mess that I've made, not only in my life, but in the lives of many others including family, friends, exes, employers, and even strangers…Heavenly Father let me be a continuous light that shines Your love…. Not to influence with my talents, opinions, or words, but with Your truth, love, and Grace!

I ask you to wash me, and cleanse me with your precious blood…forgive me of any sin that I have knowingly, and unknowingly committed…I pray Lord God that I release to You any struggles, temptation, lustful thoughts, greed, envy, jealousy, and other thoughts of perversion….I bind, renounce, rebuke, and cast out of my life any form of addiction, anger, and rebellion I have made idols of in the past…I know that I am not defined by my past, but I am a new creation, who deserves a second chance at life, a pure, clean, and recovered life…I pray that You open my heart to truly seeing my enemies as my brothers, and sisters who You love just as much as me…

I ask for You to turn my stony heart, to heart of flesh…soften it, and allow me to love like You love, for my heart to break for whatever hurts You…to forgive the way You have forgiven me, and continue to stay on the path with a purpose, and plans You have mapped out for my life… I renounce every bit of witchcraft, addiction to some substance including crystal meth, alcohol, other drugs including nicotine, even psych meds, I pray to come off of….I surrender my eating disorders including anorexia, and bulimia…I renounce any act of sexual immorality including homosexuality, pornography, masturbation, and other sexual impure thoughts…

I pray that you replace these things with new actions, thoughts, and habits of holiness, and righteousness…Heavenly Father, I ask You to allow me to reconcile with my father, bringing us a closer relationship…I know that I am not destined to hold onto the past, and how we hurt each other, but I am called to move on, and to rise above the hurts being able to love, and forgive by showing the true heart of gratitude, love, and true peace that surpasses all understanding of who You are…I also pray that you continue to strengthen the bond between my mother, and I….

Please allow me to help her the way that she's always helped me, whether it be finances, physically, or emotionally…let me be there for her to be the proud son she deserves…I pray Lord God, that You allow me to forgive all of my exes that I have hurt, and that have hurt me…I ask You to break, rebuke, bind, cast out, and renounce any soul tie between us…this is not any kind of relationship that you have planned for me, or for them…I pray that You continue to keep me on the path of sobriety, and celibacy to choose a relationship with You over anyone or anything this fallen world has to offer…I also ask Lord God, to renew my mind, my thoughts, and my heart to one day seek, and be blessed with a wife, and a woman of God…I ask You Heavenly Father to bless me with children to leave a legacy that shows nothing less than a man after Your own heart…

Finally, I pray that I put down every hang up, lie, stronghold, disappointment, and resentment to leave it at the foot of the cross, never to pick it up again! I will not grow weary in doing good because I know this is my season, and the harvest is here, because I have not given up! I know that no weapons formed against me will ever prosper, and I know that I can do all things through You who gives me strength, because You work all things together for the good of those who truly love You, and seek You…

I promise to continue to seek You, in every victory, in every trial, and seek Your kingdom and Your righteousness, above all things…trusting that You will bless me with not what my flesh selfishly wants, but with everything that my spirit needs…I know that obedience is better than sacrifice, and I promise to do everything that I can to never let go of Your hand…to love You always, until the day I die…To know, that no matter how hard things get, I WILL keep Holding on, and never give up!

love You, I ask you to bless me, my family, my friends and mentors Jen and Tyler, my Pastors, my sponsor, even my enemies…Please continue to grow my heart, grow my relationship with You above all things…fill my cup with blessing, fresh anointing favor, good health, finances, and let this new life gratefully overflow new wine upon everyone I come in contact with…never let me forget where I've come from, let me always keep my eye on where You are taking me, and never let me think that I'm better than anybody else…let me always bring others up with me, as I walk with you increase as I decrease let me remain to be teachable, and put down anything that You don't want in my life…

I love You, I praise You, I worship You, and I fully surrender everything that is not of You…remove any other idols that have hindered my path…grow my hear, keep me compassionate, and loving in Jesus mighty name Heavenly Father, I ask You today to create a new heart within me. Thank You for allowing me to discern the difference between right, and wrong allowing me the conviction to repent and carry out the right decision. God thank You for letting me be honest, and no longer manipulate.

Amen!

Sanity

[#Devotional #Recovery #Trust #Faith #Hope #MentalHealth]

We end up in an insane state of life by one bad decision at a time…
We must come out of denial and hold onto hope!
Break the cycle, believe, and receive!
We must believe that there is a power greater than us that can restore us to sanity!
Trust God, step out, and break the cycle so that you can move from hurt to hope,
and from pain to gain…
What is ruling, and dominating your life today? God or chaos!
Sanity is wholeness of mind, and making decisions based on truth!
The enemy wants us to think that we cannot recover…
Sanity is…
Strength
Acceptance
New Life
Integrity
Trust
Your Higher Power
Your weakness is intended to be when you end, and God begins…
This is a no judgement zone where all are accepted!
It takes a lifetime to build integrity, and only a single bad decision to destroy it!
A half truth is a whole lie…
Stop being concerned, and fearful of what others think of you!
Let go, and let God!
Stop being concerned about tomorrow….Live for today!

Amends

[#JournalEntry #Forgiveness #Apology]

Wow, it has it been a crazy season reaching out to you because feeling in my spirit you're still upset at me, and holding offense, and disappointment towards me….I'm praying this isn't the case, and maybe I am overreacting and analyzing too much like always….The last I saw you at the meeting on Sunday, and you gave me a hug as I ran out upset, offended, and embarrassingly immature…when you gave me a hug, it showed endearment, but yet I've tried to reach out to you a few times, and I've gotten nothing from you as a response…

I'd like to apologize to you again, for blowing up, in anger, disappointment, frustration, and any disrespect I have shown…my walk isn't perfect, and I'm still learning how to handle situations new in recovery…I know I probably messed up a lot of things, and didn't show to your standards, but I apologize, and have repented to God, and He forgives me…

God sees my heart, and He loves me, and I hope you do too…love you friend, I hope you're having a great weekend!

It takes me a lot to learn with a lot of grace, and trust…I hope you see how much I really am trying I've done everything that I can to turn my life around even when things happen happen the way that I thought that they were going to I have still stayed here trying to be as joyful as possible and embrace change…

God bless you!

XO, PQ

Getting Through the Storms

[#ChurchNotes #Devotional #Recovery #Trust #Fear #Faith #Hope #MentalHealth]

Where's your dependency…upon self, or the Holy Spirit?
We must take time out to discipline ourselves to spend time with God..
Then it turns into a desire, and a delight!
Storms of life come, but don't be afraid!
We shouldn't panic..
Fear is…
False
Evidence
Appearing
Real
We need to move in love, and power, and have a sound mind…
Trust God in the storm…God gets a hold of us in the storm…
When we truly trust in God, we will step out!
Do not doubt, but have faith in the one who can move the mountain!
Move when God has you move, and stay when He says to stay…
Faith must be tested..
Keep your eyes on Jesus…
Don't ever let your emotions get the best of you!
Even if your faith falters, Christ is always there!
Storms can help us in many ways….storms can rejuvenate you!

Don't Give the Enemy a Seat In Your Mind (Trauma)

[#ChurchNotes #Devotional #Recovery #Trust #Fear #Faith #Hope #MentalHealth]

Sometimes it's drama, but sometimes it's trauma!
Trauma isn't something we make up, it's something we experience…
There are things that happened to you, and through you that have caused trauma in someone else…
We are a new creation, but we have to renew our minds…
When you feel trauma has you stuck in a moment, let the peace of God get you out of it!
Don't let the enemy rob you from God who wants to heal you…
He can turn your trauma and make beauty from ashes…
TIME- doesn't make it all go away. Don't buy into the lie that time heals all wounds of trauma.
REVEAL- to heal. If you don't reveal your trauma, you will continue to live it over and over again…
ADMIT- you need help! Allow your trauma the chance to be healed by admitting it…
UNLOCK- the power to change, and turn away from trauma…
MAKE- community a priority….Everybody's walk needs to be met with strong community!
ACCEPT- Jesus…His love is the only remedy to heal trauma!
Stop buying the lie that you are the problem….Get the help you need to deal with your trauma, and overcome it!
Don't stay stuck in a moment of trauma, get out of it…
Ignoring trauma will not help you…
Don't let anyone ever minimize your trauma..

Believing a Lie Rewires Your Brain

[#ChurchNotes #Devotional #Recovery #Trust #Fear #Faith #Hope #MentalHealth]

God will help you out when you can't help yourself…
You can change your mind, but only God can change your heart…
What we think shapes who we are…
Ask God to bring to light the lie I keep believing over, and over…
This isn't self improvement, it's God improvement!
You can't change what you don't confront..
How do you change perspective? You confront the lie, and replace it with truth!
Satan knows our name, but calls us out on what we did…
Remember Satan is the enemy….We fight each other because of the lies we hear…
Perception is reality….Take inventory on your thoughts!
If it's a lie, replace it with the truth!
Don't continue to focus on your problems….Be grateful!
By focusing on the problem, you continue to fall for the lies!
Change your perception, and focus on the big picture…
We cannot control what happens to us….But, we can change how we perceive it!
You will change your perspective through prayer, and praise!
Everything you need is in God's presence!
It's easy enough to get overwhelmed….Remember God is enough!
To change perspective takes discipline…
If God calls you, He will provide!
Let God change your thinking….It will change your life!

Inventory Taking a Self Evaluation….

[#ChurchNotes #Devotional #Recovery #Trust #Fear #Faith #Hope #MentalHealth]

What does it look like? It starts inwardly…
Romans 12:3
Do not think of yourself higher than you are..
How is your spiritual appetite?
Do nothing out of selfish ambition or vain conceit…
Enjoy your Christianity and find balance…
Searching inward, onward, and upward..
Search me O' God and change the things I can't see!
Trust in the Holy Spirit to take you through the process…
Be of service!
Be honest with yourself…
Sometimes things don't happen right away, but continue to press on…
Stay focused on your mission.. Don't throw in the towel, you're on assignment!
Stay in the race….It's a marathon, not a sprint!
Ask God for three areas to help you in…
Spiritual
Relationships
Finances

Light and Dark

[#ChurchNotes #Devotional #Recovery #Trust #Fear #Faith #Hope #MentalHealth]

We must watch out for false teachers!
Darkness is defined as dimness, and obscurity…. Something that is concealed…
Darkness always tries to hide what the light is trying to bring out…
Pride hides…It keeps us, and tempts us from telling the truth!
Darkness summed up in these three things…
Lust of the flesh
Lust of the eyes
Pride of life
It is the trick of the enemy to get us to walk in darkness!
Lust, pride, greed, envy….
You can't be walking in sin, and salvation at the same time….#Facts
If you are walking in darkness, you can't be a child of light…
Unless your nature and desires change, you are not saved!
Children walking in the light will be convicted by the Holy Spirit..
God is light, and in Him there is no darkness…
Definition of light is a ray that's bright, and shines like fire!
Darkness doesn't have the power to suppress light…
When you walk in light, freedom will follow…
Let your light shine before men, so it brings glory to our Father in Heaven….
God is light!

Love is the expression of light..
You know you are walking in light, when you display love for one another..,
Don't confuse love with weakness…
The hater's have nothing to do with your destiny!
He who abides in God abides in love…
Any battle you address with love is success…
No fear in love….Perfect love casts out all fear!
We loved Him, because He first loved us…
If you say you love God, and can't love your brother…. The truth isn't in you!
The light changes, and illuminates us….It brings the desires of your heart!
You can choose light, or darkness….The choice is yours…

Victory

[#ChurchNotes #Devotional #Recovery #Trust #Fear #Faith #Hope #MentalHealth]

Apart from God we can do nothing….With Him we can do all things!
Humble yourself, trust, and surrender to God, and He will lift you up…
How to have victory over defects of character
V-oluntarily submit to God
I-dentify character defects to work on first
C-hange your mind
T-urning character defects over to Jesus Christ
O-ne day at a time
R-ecovery is a process
Y-ou must choose to change

Staying the Course (Relentless Pursuit)

[#ChurchNotes #Devotional #Recovery #Trust #Fear #Faith #Hope #MentalHealth]

Remain faithful despite all of life's trials, and struggles!
The call of God is irrevocable…
The only one who can short change the calling of God on our lives, is us!
We need to be a faithful steward with what God gives us…
The evidence of desire is pursuit..
Commitment is to be dedicated to a cause or activity…
We need to be committed the cause!
If God called you to it, He will see you through it!
Philippians 3:10

Transformed (Devil not today)

[#ChurchNotes #Devotional #Recovery #Trust #Fear #Faith #Hope #MentalHealth]

Every time the enemy comes into your life, doesn't always have to be a bad thing…. It's meant to strengthen you, and equip you, giving you spiritual wisdom, and knowledge!

Beware, and pay attention to false prophets, and wolves in sheep's clothing…

Those that do evil hate the light…. That's when your family shows hate towards you….When you come to Christ, you are the light, and the darkness from the world will hate you…

He that comes to the light will be pulled from the darkness with a purpose, and a destiny!

Every time the devil hides what he is doing in darkness, he speaks on what you used to do, and who you used to be….God then takes those words from the enemy to assist, and mold you into your destiny!

You are a new creation, and shall not walk in shame and guilt…

We are transformed to bring God glory!

To be transformed is to change the outward appearance, and your character, and condition…

Finally, remember what the enemy said about you. Jesus has already paid the price on the cross…

The Truth About Shame

[#ChurchNotes #Devotional #Recovery #Trust #Fear #Faith #Hope #MentalHealth]

Shame is reinforced by behavior, and hiding…

Freshwater, and salt water cannot coexist…. Shame is the salt water, God's truth is the freshwater!

You can't think your way out of shame, you have to experience your way out through vulnerability…

Until you tell the whole story, shame will tell the story of you…

Find someone you can trust to help you through shame…. Must be someone who's story is not similar….

Shame can block your true identity…

Let the Holy Spirit carry your true identity…. Not the burdens shame declares you are by bad choices…

The real you is who God says you are…

Shame is a liar, and a thief…

When you fall, and slip….That's not the real you….It's the dead you that youShame comes in many forms of depression, anxiety, and insecurities…

Truly be in the light of community….

It's not about performance to get out of shame…

Perfectionism leads you up for another bout of shame…

Don't hold your story back….Be as transparent, and vulnerable as you continue to carry…

Confess your sins to one another so that you can experience freedom, and be healed!

Character & Integrity

[#ChurchNotes #Devotional #Recovery #Trust #Fear #Faith #Hope #MentalHealth]

Be quick to listen, slow to speak. Think before you react. Look to God's word for wisdom and truth. Careful not to air out your own opinions. Lead people to Christ, not self or the world.

Careful to speak life, and not death. Compliment and not complain. Repent daily for anger.

Trust in leadership, and teachers. Lean not on my own understanding.

Guard your heart. Its actions flow from the mouth. Be anxious about nothing. Tomorrow has its own worries.

Your speech says a lot about your character and integrity. Without love your words fall flat.

Praying continuously for God's peace that surpasses all understanding. A peaceful heart is a God fearing heart.

Stay humble, and open to correction and remain teachable. Service to others.

Listen and not just speak, you are not always right.

Live through love. Love is action. Forgive all because I have been forgiven.

8 Golden Rules

[#ChurchNotes #Devotional #Recovery #Trust #Fear #Faith #Hope #MentalHealth]

Stay connected to the truth God's word.
Never compromise my convictions.
Hold my recovery high priority,
take care of myself to be strong enough to care for others.
Stay grateful in all things.
If you fall and fail, don't stay stuck.
Fail means…First Attempt In Learning!
Let God carry me when I am tired.
Let go of control, let Jesus take the wheel.

Compromising our Convictions….

[#ChurchNotes #Devotional #Recovery #Trust #Fear #Faith #Hope #MentalHealth]

We need to…Re-position, Re-fire, and Rejuvenate!

Stand firmly on the Word of God!

Genesis 13:10-13

We need to be totally committed to Christ!

Be careful when you chase money, and things….The love for money is the root of all evil…

"Seek first the Kingdom of God, and His righteousness….All things will be added upon your life!" Matthew 6:33

In life, we are given many choices…. Lean on God to lead you on the path of the right choice!

When you start making choices in the wrong direction, you pitch your tent on unhealthy, and unholy ground…

Where are you pitching your tent?

Isaiah 54:2-3 NKJV

"Enlarge the place of your tent, And let them stretch out the curtains of your dwellings; Do not spare; Lengthen your cords, And strengthen your stakes. For you shall expand to the right and to the left, And your descendants will inherit the nations, And make the desolate cities inhabited."

Obedience Is Better Than Sacrifice

[#ChurchNotes #Devotional #Recovery #Trust #Fear #Faith #Hope #MentalHealth]

When obedient to God, the blessings come so does opposition….
We can't control what happens to us, but we can control how we handle, and react to it
Take focus off of self to help others…
Truly walk in humility….What good are gifts, talents, and power if you have a prideful heart, and don't operate in love?
Taking the limits off God
When you let go, and let GOD….You're in for the ride of your life!
Little is much in the hands of God….Release what is in your hands!
Take the limitations off of God, and let the blessings flow!
Get rid of that old way of thinking, and let God transform your mind!
Don't hinder the blessings of God by putting limitations on God….Walk in your anointing!
Where's your faith level?
Step out in obedience!
God is the rewarder of those who diligently seek Him!
Don't let doubt prevent God from doing miracles in your life!

Coming Out of the Night, and into the Light…

[#ChurchNotes #Devotional #Recovery #Trust #Fear #Faith #Hope #MentalHealth]

Stop hiding….You don't have to be afraid of God!
God is Holy, and cannot dwell in darkness…
A little bit of sin messes everything up….#FACTS
James 5:16 Confess your sins to one another…
Stop living in denial…
Four areas to uncover..

Your mind….Take your thoughts captive to Jesus Christ! The most difficult thing to open up is a closed mind….Have you guarded your mind in the past? Have you filled your mind with inappropriate movies, music, and internet sites? Straight living can't come from crooked thinking! #MikeDrop
Have you failed to concentrate on the truth of the scriptures? You can't know God intimately without the Word of God! #TruthBomb
God owns your body….Take care of it….It's a temple for the Holy Spirit! What activities, or habits contribute to your body?
Have you mistreated anyone in your family? Feel the weight of your sin! Stop torturing your loved ones if you want to stay stuck in your mess….Who in your family do you have resentments with?
Who do you owe amends to? What is my part in the damaged relationship? What family secrets do you hold onto? Have you been faithful to your church? Have you been critical or active? Choose to be the change! Have you discouraged your family from church?
Keep accountability, and community close…

Lean Not on Your Own Understanding

[#ChurchNotes #Devotional #Recovery #Trust #Fear #Faith #Hope #MentalHealth]

Submit to the Word of God, and lean not on your own understanding!

The Bible is a buffet, the five-fold ministry!
A Christian must walk in love... Agape love...
1 Corinthians 13
If you're not walking in the love of God, everything you do is in vain!
We must walk in the Spirit, and deny the flesh!
Control your thought life...An idle mind is the devil's playground!
Quit complaining, and focus on what is going right!
Worry more about your heart, than your talent...
Rebuke pride and offense in the name of Jesus!
Think of things that will build you up, not tear you down...
Put on everything in Jesus, and in love!

Prophesy a Mind Shift to a Life Shift

[#ChurchNotes #Devotional #Recovery #Trust #Fear #Faith #Hope #MentalHealth]

A prophetic word shifts things...
A prophetic word changes seasons...
A prophetic word brings things to LIFE, and brings things to DEATH within us
A prophetic word creates a beginning, and also establishes an end...
"The End"
Breaking bondages and addictions!
It's a new season! Time to create a beginning and an end to things that are destined in our lives!
This includes relationships, jobs, and lifestyle
Declare, and decree that Jesus is in control...
There will never be a change, unless you rebel against the things contrary to the word of God!
The devil doesn't let go easily, or give up any territory...
But today, he's losing the fight!
Keep going… Don't give up!

Realignment

[#ChurchNotes #Devotional #Recovery #Trust #Fear #Faith #Hope #MentalHealth]

God promises a greater glory if we obey...
We are the temple of the Holy Spirit!
We need to shift our focus, and align our values with His...
God is calling us to realign today!
Blessings come to your home, when you concentrate on building God's temple!
God has a calling on our lives...
We are a Remnant for God!
Obedience, Preparation, Willingness
When God asks us to go, or let go we need to obey!
This means walking away from situations, even unhealthy relationships
A new normal could be a new task
Focus on the positive new lifestyle, task, or place God has called us to
As followers of Jesus, we should prepare for that, surrender, and obey!

Die 2 Our Flesh (Fear Not)

[#ChurchNotes #Devotional #Recovery #Trust #Fear #Faith #Hope #MentalHealth]

Live to be rooted in Christ, and don't allow fear to take over
When we die to self, people's words and actions cannot harm us
Failure is part of life...Learn from it!
Remember fail means…
First
Attempt
In
Learning
Don't deny Jesus like Peter did when the pressure is on!
Are you in your word, and praying or seeking advice from others?
Build up your 401K in Christ, and store up your treasures in Heaven!
Every day we must…
Die to sin
Tame the tongue
Die to the flesh
What are you willing to do for God?
We must decrease, so He can increase!
Rely on God and not man...Focus on His will!

Rise Up

[#ChurchNotes #Devotional #Recovery #Trust #Fear #Faith #Hope #MentalHealth]

Grace is not just a huge blanket to cover your repetitive sin...
God wants a changed heart!
Friendship with the world is an enemy of God!
We can rise above every situation if we hide, and abide in Jesus!
We can't live in the same old same old...
Let the Holy Spirit revolutionize your life!
Let go, and let God!
Cut the cord to the wagon of sin you keep pulling behind you!
Rise up in Jesus!

Don't Fall (the Bait of Satan)

[#ChurchNotes #Devotional #Recovery #Trust #Fear #Faith #Hope #MentalHealth]

Me offended
The closer the relationship the more severe the offense...
Only those you care about can hurt you...
Our response to offense becomes our future...
Two Categories of offended people...
People who have been treated unjustly
People who believe they've been treated badly...
Pride keeps you from admitting your condition of offense...
Pride allows you to justify offense...
In the heat of trials impurities show up...
Either remain angry, or repent...
See your true heart condition...
When we see ourselves as victims, we justify ourselves for being angry and bitter...
You will only repent when you see your true condition, and stop blaming others...

Massive Offense
End days = Many offended
Without God, we can only love with a selfish love (non-agape)
Develop faith in the love of God...
He who sows to the flesh will reap corruption...

But he who sows to the spirit, will reap everlasting life!
Galatians 6:8-9
We need faith in the Father's love to truly forgive others...
When you sow to the spirit, and love others freely, don't get offended and upset if they don't love you back...
When our expectations aren't met, we walk in selfish love, and ambition...
When you have expectations on people, they can let you down...But if you don't have expectations on someone, anything given is a blessing!
The more we expect, the greater potential offense!
When we filter everything through past hurts, rejections, and experiences we find it impossible to believe God...We doubt His goodness
This causes us to again justify ourselves instead of repent...
False prophets...Must be identified by their fruit, not their teachings...
They will tell people what they want to hear, not what they need to hear...
They may boast, but not have the character of Christ...
They will have a zeal for knowledge, but remain unchanged by God's power and never apply it...
Always learning but never coming to the truth
2 Timothy 3:7
Stop running from church to church to escape offense!
Repent, and be free from your deception and offense, you self seeking generation of hypocrites! It doesn't matter how up to date you are, how many books you've read, seminars you've been to, or how many hours you've prayed and studied...
If you are offended, unforgiving, and refuse to repent, you have not come to the knowledge of the truth...

You are deceived, and confuse others with your hypocritical lifestyle! No matter what the revelation, your fruit tells a different story!
You become a spring spewing out bitter waters that will bring deception not truth...
Offense leads to betrayal... Betrayal leads to hatred...
When we betray we seek our own benefit at the expense of others...Usually someone whom you're in relation with...
The closer the relationship, the more severe the betrayal...
To betray someone is the ultimate abandonment of a covenant...
Unless genuine repentance follows, the relationship cannot be restored...
Betrayal then leads to hatred with serious consequences...
Notes taken from "Bait of Satan" by, John Bevere

Into the Deep

[#ChurchNotes #Devotional #Recovery #Trust #Fear #Faith #Hope #MentalHealth]

What it means to say yes to God...
Do you change the world around you?
When you say yes to God, it changes the hardest of hearts, and changes the world around you!
Being good doesn't solve the problem of sin...Being forgiven by God's grace does... Simply say, "God please forgive me!"
Proximity to Jesus means distance to sin...
When you say yes, the power of God transcends everything around you...
It changes you, and the world around you...
We're all called to be righteous, and Holy saints to follow Jesus...
If you've never been invited? Call out to Him and pray...
Don't hold back...What good is it to gain the world, and lose your soul?
Help me to give a complete yes to you, and be a light in the darkness!

Don't let barriers of woundedness stop you from praying, and communing with God...
Mental prayer is important to keep us close to Jesus...
It's not prideful to aim for what God aims for us to do, because it's His will...
In the end, we want to hear, "Well done!" Not because I'm good, but because He made me good...
Prayer is a never ending journey to the heart of God...
Necessary elements for successful prayer...
Sacred Space
Sacred Time
Sacred Attention
Necessary Conditions for dramatic Spiritual growth...
Clarity
Community
Accountability
Spiritual Direction

Notes from Dan Burke, "Into the Deep"

The Fruit You Bear

[#ChurchNotes #Devotional #Recovery #Trust #Fear #Faith #Hope #MentalHealth]

Take action instead of just standing still...
Live your life out loud reproducing its fruit unto others!
Are you living for God, or for yourself?
Don't make war on others...Remember, your biggest fan, and critic is the person staring back at you in the mirror every morning...
Don't let fear hold you back from a goal you're trying to achieve!
Remember, fear stands for…

False
Evidence
Appearing
Real
Spiritual Disorientation..
When we trust our feelings, over God's Word we're gonna fail!
Remember assuming wrong affects more than just you...
Sin has drastic consequences, so we must take drastic measures to avoid it!
Big moments start with little decisions...

The Devil's Crockpot

[#ChurchNotes #Devotional #Recovery #Trust #Fear #Faith #Hope #MentalHealth Rated M]

Don't fall for what the devil has cooking in his crockpot!
When we walk around hungry, we make poor decisions...
That's why we need to be full of the God's Word...
Genesis 25: 24-34
Don't let your temper cost you your testimony, by giving up your birthright...
Don't let the enemy offer you a bowl of BS stew of lies from his crockpot of destruction!
Casual sex will cost you your calling!
Don't trade what you've always wanted for something you want right now...
We can't just grow up, we must mature within...
Stop being a six foot baby!
Now screams louder, but later screams longer!
Stop trading your birthright for a bowl of sin!
Stop letting the enemy pour out things like entitlement causing you to become ungrateful!
Stop letting temptation brew...
The devil cannot take your calling!
Be holy...Because without holiness, no one will see the Lord!
Don't give up everything God has for your life over one night of fleshly satisfaction!
Bitter roots can destroy your foundation!
Bitterness is a root of spiritual suicide!
We must deny ourselves, take up our crosses, and follow Jesus!
Gifting will allow you to stand before great men, but character will allow you to stand before God!

Seek His Will 2 Fulfill

[#ChurchNotes #Devotional #Recovery #Trust #Fear #Faith #Hope #MentalHealth]

There's a difference between doing something, and God calling you out to be faithful and do something...
We are living sacrifices called to live a life pointing others to Christ...
An idle mind is the devil's playground...
When you keep your hands busy in God's things, you stay focused...
We are called to be good and faithful workers!
The Lord desires us to be faithful, and carry His image with us everywhere...
Plant your feet now to work hard towards your goals...
We're not a secret society, we are called to honor God in public at work...
When you're faithful with the small things, God will give you more...
Pray, and be diligent about what God wants for your life, and stop leapfrogging God!
If you ask things outside of God's will, don't expect an answer...
Open up your Bible and, and pray...Beware of false prophets!
If you're not a model in serving others, how can you make an impact?
If you're miserable, change the lens you see things through, and see them through the lens of Christ!
We are out to make a difference with what God has given us...
You don't need a platform on center stage to make a difference, and build the Kingdom...
Even when you have a bad day, model Christ for all who is around you...
Display unselfish actions while showing the heart of Christ!
Let the way you act at work be an extension of Christ...

"Whatever you do, work at it with all your heart, as working for the Lord, not for human masters."

Prodigal Come Home

[#ChurchNotes #Devotional #Recovery #Trust #Fear #Faith #Hope #MentalHealth]

Stay away from the distant land!
When we go to the distant land, we become part of the problem...
What is stopping you from coming home to the Father?
What is stopping you, when you're invited?
The distant land is full of empty promises...
What happens if you take a plant out of its soil? It dies...
What happens if you take a fish out of water? It dies...
So what happens if we remove ourselves from the image of God? We will die spiritually!
Don't let crime, pride, anger, or greed lead you to the distant land of despair...
Sinning is going to take you further than you ever wanted to go...
Make you stay longer than you ever wanted to stay...
And make you pay more than you were ever willing to pay!
God desires a relationship with each, and every single one of us waiting at the porch with open arms...
He doesn't see labels, He has a calling for your life...
You have a story, you are invited! Come home to Jesus!
The door is open...

Let it Go

[#ChurchNotes #Devotional #Recovery #Trust #Fear #Faith #Hope #MentalHealth]

Keep less of what doesn't matter, keep more of what does…

Your stuff doesn't define you…

Better to have one hand full of what matters, than two hands that don't…

If you have something that's weighing you down, toss it!

Don't let things weigh you down, and steal your joy…

Don't hold onto it, bless somebody else who needs it…

Buy less!

Give it away if you have way more than enough to give…

Donate it!

Don't let your lack of faith in thinking you might need it later allow you to hold onto it now…

Toss it!

If you accumulate stuff only to enrich yourself, you will enter into eternity empty handed…

Give more!

With great wealth comes great responsibility…

What are you willing to give?

Joy is not found in receiving, but in giving…

Christmas is about the birth of our Savior, and serving others…Not about getting stuff!

Your stuff doesn't define who you are…Your relationship with Christ, and others do!

Don't Get Caught Up

[#ChurchNotes #Devotional #Recovery #Trust #Fear #Faith #Hope #MentalHealth]

~Never let the urgent overtake the important!~

It is important to pray...Don't let the urgent distractions of the world stop you from praying...

If you're going to leave a legacy, spend time doing things that matter...

Don't use your time to be popular, or famous...

God doesn't say, "Well done my good, and famous servant!" We've gotta be faithful!

Don't give up what you want most, for what you want right now...

"Regularly tending to the minor urgency of life, will limit your ability to NURTURE the important things that matter the most."

Good things are not always God things...

The body suffers when you get caught up in the urgent, and ignore the important!

Do a 180, and turn around and give it to Jesus!

A Good Leader is a God Leader

[#ChurchNotes #Devotional #Recovery #Trust #Fear #Faith #Hope #MentalHealth]

Characteristics of a great leader!

Some people live lives as victims instead of victorious...

We must go from leadership potential to leadership of God's people!

Let God deal with the Goliath in your life to emerge a leader...

Being a leader is not a profession, but a debt to pay the Lord back for rescuing our lives...

Have strong convictions instead of compromising your values...

A good leader, elevates others above self!

In Spirit and in Truth

[#ChurchNotes #Devotional #Recovery #Trust #Fear #Faith #Hope #MentalHealth]

Study the devil's techniques and fight back the enemy in Spirit during spiritual warfare!

Put on the full armor of God for protection!

The Armor of God Ephesians 6:10-18

Finally, be strong in the Lord and in his mighty power. Put on the full armor of God, so that you can take your stand against the devil's schemes. For our struggle is not against flesh and blood, but against the rulers, against the authorities, against the powers of this dark world and against the spiritual forces of evil in the heavenly realms.

Therefore, put on the full armor of God, so that when the day of evil comes, you may be able to stand your ground, and after you have done everything, to stand. Stand firm then, with the belt of truth buckled around your waist, with the breastplate of righteousness in place, and with your feet fitted with the readiness that comes from the gospel of peace. In addition to all this, take up the shield of faith, with which you can extinguish all the flaming arrows of the evil one. Take the helmet of salvation and the sword of the Spirit, which is the word of God.

And pray in the Spirit on all occasions with all kinds of prayers and requests. With this in mind, be alert and always keep on praying for all the Lord's people.

Know your enemy is the devil, and not man...
Be sober minded and vigilant because the adversary the devil is like a roaring lion...
If you want to win the fight, study his moves...
We've got the power to back away from sin!

Don't Look Back

[#ChurchNotes #Devotional #Recovery #Trust #Fear #Faith #Hope #MentalHealth]

Jesus isn't looking for an emotional decision, but a lifelong decision!
We come to church to get crafted and molded into His image...
Luke 9:23 Deny yourself...
John 6:66 Don't turn away from Christ...
When you deny yourself, you refuse to associate with self...
Spiritual maturity is serving God's agenda...
As a follower of Christ, you should never look back!
If you look back, you'll go back...
If you have no vision for your life, you'll always go back to what you know!

Mind Management

[#Church Notes #Devotional #Recovery #Trust #Fear #Faith #Hope #MentalHealth]

The battle always starts in the mind...
Whatever gets in your mind gets you...
Learn how to guard your mind, and strengthen your mind...
Train your brain...
Romans 12:2
My thoughts control my life...
My mind is a battleground for sin...
My mind is the key to peace...
Don't believe everything you think...
Guard your mind from garbage...
Pray as much as you worry...
Be a disciplined disciple...
Become a lifelong learner...
A person without vision for their lives will always go back to what they know...
Five Levels of Learning
Knowledge
Wisdom
Conviction
Character
Skilled
Stretch your imagination
Our gift from God is our life...
Our gift back to God is what we do with our life...
Start dreaming big, and don't let the lies come in to destroy you...
Romans 14:23 Everything that does not come from faith is sin...

Come Follow Me

[#ChurchNotes #Devotional #Recovery #Trust #Fear #Faith #Hope #MentalHealth]

Imitate Me (Jesus), cause I don't wanna lose you...
The biggest failure in church is not being able to make disciples...
Those that do not want to imitate anything, won't produce anything...
When people are free to do as they please, they usually imitate others...
No man fails on purpose...But we also don't succeed by accident...
Matthew 28:19-20
Disciple is a learner...
Fully committed to obey Jesus at any cost...
God's Word is about transformation...
We need to go from curious to convinced...
Then from convinced to committed...
If you're not imitating Christ...
The essence of discipleship is relationship...
Building people with the word of God is discipleship...
You need 3 types of people
Barnabas, a peer…
Paul, someone pouring into your life mentoring you...
Timothy, someone you're pouring into...
Ephesians 4:1...By being a disciple you must be an example...
Walk worthy of the call you have received...
You have to make God's agenda your agenda...
We must be doers of the Word...
James 2:14
There has to be works coming from your faith...

2 Timothy 2:2

Seasons

[#ChurchNotes #Devotional #Recovery #Trust #Fear #Faith #Hope #MentalHealth]

There's a Time and a Season For Everything
Trust in God throughout all Seasons.
Growing Season
Pruning Season
The Mountain Season
The Wilderness Season
The Harvest Season
Let God stop you, and shape you to become what He needs you to become!

How are you going to respond?
Embrace the season you're in...
When a season comes, change!
God knows where you're going...
Your destination is always influenced by what you're willing to leave...
Philippians 1:6
God WILL complete the work He's began!

Soul Winner

[#ChurchNotes #Devotional #Recovery #Trust #Fear #Faith #Hope #MentalHealth]

Turning ordinary moments into eternal moments...
Grace gives you the ability to look good while going through trials...
When we lose the passion to see others won over to the Lord, we lose Jesus...
Living for the cause is dying for their selfishness...
Four things in being a soul winner...
Enjoy Christ yourself...Don't just acknowledge Christ...Know Him!
Philippians 4:6-7...
Matthew 6:34...
Don't worry, but trust in God...
1 Peter 5:7...
If I trust God, I can enjoy God...
John 14:1...
Letting your hearts be troubled is a choice...
Pray regularly...
Proclaim it clearly...
2 Timothy 2:15...
Live Wisely...
1 Peter 3:9...

Act Like You're Saved

[#ChurchNotes #Devotional #Recovery #Trust #Fear #Faith #Hope #MentalHealth]

We need to do what we say we're going to do...It's called character...
We have all been engraved with character impressions...we all have issues...
How do we deal with life?
Here are Five F's to be saved...
Focus...
Faithful...
Fruitful...
Forgiving...
Friendly...
Good habits, good discipline...Bad habits, bad discipline...
Get unstuck...Stop being stuck on stupid and doing your own thing...
God is more concerned about your character than your comfort...
God builds our character...
God allows pressure to come, because pressure builds character...
You're either a soldier or civilian...
Be loyal to the cause...
Learn how to endure pain to go to the next level...
1 Timothy 6 11-12
It's a choice to flee...
Any breakdown in life can be caused by a breakdown in character...
James 21:21-22
Qualities to being a good Christian...
Train your brain...
Have holiness in your life is a choice...
Never let success get to your head, or failure to get into your heart...
Know why we're here, and what asset we can bring...
One positive thing about everyone in the room...
Team Building experiment for next week...

Magnify Your Moments

[#ChurchNotes #Devotional #Recovery #Trust #Fear #Faith #Hope #MentalHealth]

Romans 10:10
Faith is action!!! You cannot just believe, you've gotta move...
If you're not challenging faith, you're not pleasing God...
God meets our needs via opportunities...
Seize our opportunities...
Procrastination is equated to low self-esteem...
Be intentional in leading your life, and stop accepting it!!!
Take your eyes off of your situation, and put them on God...
Seek opportunities from God...
The size of your dreams should be the size of your God!!!
Most people don't lead their lives, they except their lives...
When God closes one door, He opens
Look for God in opportunities, and trust God to take care of you!!!

You Reap What You Sow

[#ChurchNotes #Devotional #Recovery #Trust #Fear #Faith #Hope #MentalHealth]

Laws of man, and law of God...
We are where we're at because of the choices we make...
Make changes today for your tomorrow to change...
Every choice has a consequence...
Ephesians 5:5-7...
The key is not giving up...We have two choices:
the Spirit, or the flesh...
Either you're serving God or the enemy...God or yourself...
Everything you do today determines your future...
You reap what you sow...
How do you handle the no's of life? Die to your flesh...
There are no shortcuts...This is God's law...
God will not be mocked!
God allows you to go through the same things over and over....
Until you pass the test…Go through the process!
The more you're obedient, the more freedom you get...
The more you understand, the more you surrender, the more God will use you...
Trust God, and take a step of faith...
Sow to the Spirit, and please God...
If you sow to the Spirit, expect for God to reward you...

Don't give up!!! Be obedient, and active in the Spirit of God...
Grow up in God, and stop worrying about why others are so privileged...
Worry about others instead of yourself...
Let others be blessed, and shine...Stop worrying about yourself...
Sow into the Spirit...
2 Corinthians 9:6-7...
When you refresh others, you too will be refreshed...
When you share the things God's given you...That's what God wants!!!
Disciple men, and pass it on...Sow into the Spirit, and don't hold on until later...
You reap what you sow...

10 Keys (Next Level)

[# ChurchNotes #Devotional #Recovery #Trust #Fear #Faith #Hope #MentalHealth]

When God's preparing you for a new level, make sure you have everything you need to move to the next level...

Be convinced of the call...When you know you're called nothing can convince you otherwise...When you're not convinced of your call, you will focus on the problems...Only a deep conviction of your call will keep you going...

Realize that a prophetic word is not enough...Hear God speak in your heart personally...Always look for confirmation first...Do not wait too long when you receive your confirmation to move...

Consider how God has used you in the past...Allow your past experiences and successes propel you into the future!! He is equipping you to your next level...

Determine how you must change...The change must take place in the present for this new season...You must be actively involved in worship, reading, and praying...Be equipped to move to your new level...

Commit to overcoming the opposition...As God moves you forward, the enemy wants to keep you stuck or make you move backwards...The higher the levels, the higher the devils....Being too comfortable (complacent) will keep you from getting to the next level...

Build a mentoring relationship...Don't ever feel weak when you need help...

Being aligned with the right mentor, will help you grow...This relationship can be vital to get to the next level...

Be prepared for increased spiritual attacks...The more you move in the process, the more effective you will be for the Kingdom, and more of a threat you become to the enemy...2 Corinthians 2:14...When you step up, the battles will heat up...New battles require new strategies...In Christ you have spiritual armor (Ephesians)...Through attacks you will overcome with God's help!!

Accept acceptance...When you step into it, you will step into the anointing...Don't let false humility creep in...A humble person doesn't try to explain their own opinions, give Him glory.in all things...Trust His wisdom, and follow His lead...Don't become proud...

Remember that transition takes time...Stay encouraged, and be patient, not trying to change things on your own...Walk in step with God...His timing is perfect, and part of a great plan for your life...One step at a time, one day at a time, one victory at a time...

Move ahead with bold faith...When God is shifting you, go for it boldly with faith springing it into action putting it more into life than ever!! Always remember God is faithful in finishing the work He's done in you...Move on, and move up!!! Time to step up into that next level!!!

Brothers Keeper (SUAD)

[#ChurchNotes #Devotional #Recovery #Trust #Fear #Faith #Hope #MentalHealth]

Protect your neighbor! It's about…
Connection
Conversion
Continued Prayer
Celebration
If you're not praying, God's not providing…
Always keep your prayer life big, and trust in God…
The more you pray, the more you love people…
Stop putting expectations on people…
Lower them, and work on yourself!!!
Stop crucifying Christ, and putting Him back on the cross by your disobedience…
True worship is responding while in God's presence…
We need an active church who is involved…
Godly fulfillment is in ministry, when you see lives being changed and transformed!!!
SUAD means….
Shut
Up
And
Die
The more you give, and refresh others, the more you will be refreshed…
Discipleship is not just about salvation, but reproduction of yourself…

Lights, Camera, Action!
[#ChurchNotes #Devotional #Recovery #Trust #Fear #Faith #Hope #MentalHealth]

Rev 4:8-11
You're in dress rehearsal...What you do now is going to show what, and how you will worship Him in Heaven...
The purpose of Worship isn't to make us feel better...Don't worship in vain...
3 things worship does...
Reminds you of who God is...
Rebukes the storm you are in...
Puts the enemy in his place…
If it doesn't match this, change your worship!

Lazarus Come Forth

[#ChurchNotes #Devotional #Recovery #Trust #Fear #Faith #Hope #MentalHealth]

Lazarus represents the church falling asleep or dead...The spirit of worldliness is poisoning the body of Christ!
We need to take a stand and rise up for Jesus!!!
Proverbs 28:1
We are at war!!!
The church is sick and has been drinking poison...We have let social drinking, gambling, pornography, homosexuality, and other sin creep into the church...
Jesus isn't done with you yet so don't give up!!!
God loved you when you hated yourself!!!
God's love and power will come to you where you're at...
Get ready and stay ready...God is coming back for a church that isn't lukewarm...
Come forth with transformation, holiness, and awake Lazarus get up!!!

Blindsided

[#ChurchNotes #Devotional #Recovery #Trust #Fear #Faith #Hope #MentalHealth]

Ephesians 6 put on the full armor and remind yourself that we don't fight against flesh and blood but the spirits and principalities in the spiritual realm...
Do you feel like you have a bullseye on your back? That's because When you are called to do great things for God's Kingdom, the enemy will relentlessly attack!!!
Stay on guard, and don't feel like you're a prisoner of lost hope...
Do not look in the rear view mirror...Keep moving forward!!!
When you pray it matters, and when you don't pray it matters...
When you throw away your hope you throw away your faith also...

Third Wave

[#ChurchNotes #Devotional #Recovery #Trust #Fear #Faith #Hope #MentalHealth]

If we don't shift with the movement, we'll miss it...
When God shifts the movement...He shifts the leaders!
Position yourself in the third wave and make it personal!
There's nothing we cannot accomplish with strong leadership...
God will shift the movement to prepare us for the future!
4 things
The clarity of the vision... Clarity will bring purpose to the vision...
Look for an opportunity, not just a miracle!!!
The community of vision...
Unity is vital to the vision...Nothing can be accomplished without unity!!!
The same bricks God gives us to build with, can be the same ones we use to throw at each other...
Change is necessary to keep the vision fresh and pure...
Chemistry is important to the vision.. Motivation, moral, and momentum is needed to build ministry...
Ministry is about building people...
Leaders don't run from conflict...
God has given us a unique spirit...
We must never get away from that spirit!
The hour is now...
Although the shift is taking place, the vision will not change...
We are blessed to have leadership to protect the vision...
We stay cutting edge with 4 things....

Prayer...There will never be change without that supernatural movement of prayer... Protect the intimacy of God before anything else...

Experience and charisma can only get us so far... We need anointing and a relationship with God!

Urgency....Step out for God, and do something for God now...You cannot be a good leader in complacency... Be urgent and engage with people to take the ministry to the next level... Move with a fire inside and do something for God right now!!! Have the ability to transmit urgency to others... Don't let complacency cripple your urgency!!! Comfort is also an enemy of urgency... Let Heaven be your place of comfort... Until then stir up that fire and keep pushing forward!!! Don't become a lukewarm church...

Indifference... Stop staying in that hurt stage of self pity... Take care of your heart to stay fresh.... Are the things of God still exciting to you? Proclaim the message of Christ with intensity!!! When you serve with a sense of intensity, the things that were meant to hurt you will just bounce right off of you...

Unified vision... Be a protector of the vision... Protect your Pastors and stop gossiping!!!

Longevity... Ministry isn't easy, the devil is a liar.... Wants to put us In a place with so much depression and discouragement to want to walk away...

Don't just hear information, allow the Lord to bring transformation!!!

A setback is a setup for a comeback!

The enemy may have won the battle but we will win the war!

Never underestimate the enemy... Stay close to God, Victory Outreach, and Pastor Sonny... Don't backslide and act like you know it all...

We aren't perfect but we are willing...

United we can divided we fall..

Ever feel buried in a dark and obscure place put on a shelf? God wants to deal with your character and motives in that place!

Get on the pathway of this vision and development...

When You Win the Men You Win the War

[#ChurchNotes #Devotional #Recovery #Trust #Fear #Faith #Hope #MentalHealth]

Convictions need to be necessary...
Our convictions should come from the word of God...
Always give God your best...
Don't become cultured, convenient Christians...
If you have polluted thinking it leads to polluted living...
Holiness equals power...
A made up mind makes a difference...
We need to have convictions...
Secrets to longevity
You must have dependency on God...
We were made by a God for God...
We must work in the spirit of faith...
Get your emotions out of it...
Progression...Are we making progress as a a Christian?
Don't just go through stuff, grow through stuff!

PART 5:
FINAL REFLECTIONS FOR THE SOUL

'He heals the brokenhearted and binds up their wounds.'
PSALM 147:3

Stronger

(Lyrics by Thunderstorm Artis)

The following song lyrics, are dedicated to my beautiful mother, Rosemarie Quezada. She has been such a gift to me throughout so many trials, and victories in my life, and recovery. Many times, we have not seen eye to eye, but she has shown me the most important gift, the love of God. When I was a kid, I used to love Lynda Carter as Wonder Woman. One year for Halloween, mom dressed up as Wonder Woman and put her photograph in character on a shirt for me, to bring me joy. I have put mom through a lot of heartache, and for that I am so sorry. We cannot change our past, but we can definitely make a better future!

Call me a fool for thinkin' maybe I could get over
Or I could be stronger
Than the fear in my mind
See mama always told me I was meant to be a light
In the darkness
But I feel like a candle waiting for a flame
And she said,
"Keep on getting stronger, keep on getting wiser, my dear
Don't give in to the voices or succumb to your fears"
Oh mama, I pray, oh I pray that I'll stay strong
Oh mama, I pray, oh I pray that I'll stay strong

Mm-mm
But do you see me all low when I look to you for an answer?
I need you to tell me how to carry on
And he said,
"Keep on getting stronger, keep on getting wiser my dear
Don't give in to the voices or succumb to your fears"
Oh mama, I pray, oh I pray that I'll strong (help me stay strong)
Oh mama, I pray, I pray that I'll stay strong (help me stay strong)
Show me now if I've lost my way
I reach for freedom from within my cage
Search for meaning whenever I'm afraid
Oh mama, I pray, oh I pray that I'll strong (help me stay strong)
Oh mama, I pray, oh I pray that I'll stay strong (help me stay strong)
Oh mama, I pray, oh I pray that I'll stay strong (help me stay strong)
Oh mama, I pray, oh I pray that I'll stay strong

Or do you not know that the unrighteous will not inherit the kingdom of God? Do not be deceived: neither the sexually immoral, nor idolaters, nor adulterers, nor men who practice homosexuality, nor thieves, nor the greedy, nor drunkards, nor revilers, nor swindlers will inherit the kingdom of God.

1 Corinthians 6:9-10

Prayer to come out of Homosexuality

[#Prayer #Deliverance #Homosexuality]

Father God, I have made the decision to come out of the lifestyle that I know is an abomination in Your sight. I repent for allowing the devil to convince me to choose this lifestyle over one that is Holy, and acceptable to You. I repent for allowing the wicked desires of my flesh to have rule over me. I renounce every soul tie of every person that I've laid with in sin. I renounce the perversity of the lifestyle. I declare that I hate it because I cannot be delivered from what I love. I love the people who are bound and homosexuality, but I hate the lifestyle, it is an abomination before the Lord. I renounce the witchcraft that comes with homosexuality and lesbianism.

Father, deliver me from the shame and hurt that come with the lifestyle. Though my flesh experienced demonic pleasure, my soul was always in turmoil. I openly announce that I do not want to live a life of lies anymore. I was created to be a man. I was beautifully made in the image of God. God is not the author of confusion. I shut my ear gates to the lies of the enemy that say I was born gay, and can never be delivered. I declare once gay, not always gay. I am delivered. The perversities that I once enjoyed and allowed free passage into my mind exist no more.

Lord, I repent for going against the natural order of things. I declare the truth of Romans, which says that homosexuality and lesbianism is natural. I cast down every imagination of this lifestyle that tries to exalt itself over the knowledge of God. I understand that Your Son Jesus took on all of my sins of homosexuality on the cross, and I am redeemed Lord. I renounce everything that I participated in that seeded my soul. I renounce, gay pride, and every sign and symbol of the lifestyle. I come against the vision of the rainbow that represented a covenant between the devil and me. I renounce the language that I spoke pertaining to the lifestyle. I repent for lusting after the same sex. Fantasizing about the same sex, and engaging in any behavior with the same sex that is considered an abomination in Your sight.

Lord, I repent for setting my affections on things of this earth. Instead of things above. I repent for putting creation before my Creator. I plead the blood of Jesus Christ over my mind. God, take me from level to level, and glory to glory. I claim victory, Lord, show me how to become an advocate to cry out loudly against the homosexual agenda, and its plans, so that other men and women can be free Indeed. I declare that my body is the temple of the Holy Spirit, and the living God. I cast down homosexual desires of my heart. I know that Jeremiah 17:9 says the heart is deceitful above all things, and I do not trust my heart, I trust in Jesus! God knew what He was doing when He created me. I am a new creation in Jesus name.

Therefore, if anyone is in Christ, he is a new creation. The old has passed away; behold, the new has come.

2 Corinthians 5:17

Salvation Prayer/Sinners Prayer

[#Prayer #Deliverance #Salvation #Saved]

Step 1 – God's Purpose: Peace and Life

God loves you and wants you to experience peace and eternal life—abundant and eternal.

The Bible says:

"We have peace with God through our Lord Jesus Christ." Romans 5:1

"For God so loved the world, that He gave His one and only Son, that whoever believes in Him should not perish but have eternal life." John 3:16

"I [Jesus] came that they may have life and have it abundantly." John 10:10

Why don't most people have this peace and abundant life that God planned for us to have?

Step 2 – The Problem: Sin Separates Us

God created us in His own image to have an abundant life. He did not make us as robots to automatically love and obey Him. God gave us a will and freedom of choice. We choose to disobey God and go our own willful way. We still make this choice today. This results in separation from God.

The Bible says:

"For all have sinned and fall short of the glory of God." Romans 3:23

"For the wages of sin is death, but the free gift of God is eternal life in Christ Jesus our Lord." Romans 6:23

Our choice results in separation from God. People have tried in many ways to bridge this gap between themselves and God...

The Bible says:

"There is a way that seems right to a man, but its end is the way to death." Proverbs 14:12

"But your iniquities have made a separation between you and your God, and your sins have hidden His face from you so that He does not hear." Isaiah 59:2

No bridge reaches God... except one.

Step 3 – God's Remedy: The Cross

Jesus Christ died on the cross and rose from the grave. He paid the penalty for our sin and bridged the gap between God and people.

The Bible says:

"For there is one God, and there is one mediator between God and men, the man Christ Jesus." 1 Timothy 2:5

"For Christ also suffered once for sins, the righteous for the unrighteous, that He might bring us to God." 1 Peter 3:18

"But God shows His love for us in that while we were still sinners, Christ died for us." Romans 5:8

God has provided the only way... Each person must make a choice...

Step 4 – Our Response: Receive Christ

We must trust Jesus Christ as Lord and Savior and receive Him by personal invitation.

The Bible says:

"Behold, I stand at the door and knock. If anyone hears My voice and opens the door, I will come in to him and eat with him, and he with Me." Revelation 3:20

"But to all who did receive Him, who believed in His name, He gave the right to become children of God." John 1:12

"If you confess with your mouth that Jesus is Lord and believe in your heart that God raised Him from the dead, you will be qsaved." Romans 10:9

Will you receive Jesus Christ right now?

Here is how you can receive Christ:

Admit your need. (I am a sinner.)
Be willing to turn from your sins (repent) and ask for God's forgiveness.

Believe that Jesus Christ died for you on the cross and rose from the grave. Through prayer, invite Jesus Christ to come in and control your life through the Holy Spirit. (Receive Jesus as Lord and Savior)

i.e.
Dear God,

I know I am a sinner. I want to turn from my sins, and I ask for Your forgiveness. I believe that Jesus Christ is Your Son. I believe He died for my sins and that You raised Him to life. I want Him to come into my heart and to take control of my life. I want to trust Jesus as my Savior and follow Him as my Lord from this day forward.

In Jesus' Name, amen!

Oh God

[Worship Song Lyrics Written by: Patrick Quezada]

Oh God...Be my power...
Oh God...Be my strength...
Be the change I need...
Oh God...Be my tower...
Oh God...Be my fortress...
Be all I see...
Oh God...You're my healer...
Oh God...You're my faith...
You're my everything...
Oh God...You're my future...
Oh God...You're my Savior...
You're my destiny...
Oh God...Be the light in me...
Oh God...Live inside of me...
Oh God...You have set me free...
Oh God...You have rescued me...
Oh God...

Special Artwork

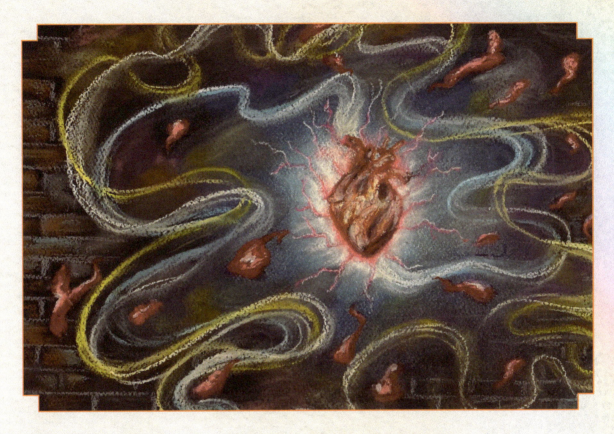

Title: *A Heart Renewed By God* | **Artist:** Victor Franco | 2022; chalk & oil pastel

I intended this piece of art to depict the renewal process God has taken Patrick through. God asked me to show the renewal and healing of the heart even through the 'walls' Patrick has faced and had to overcome throughout his life. The cleansing of the Father strips off old scar tissue to make way for the new.

Title: *Under Shadow of His Wings* | **Artist:** Victor Franco | 2022; chalk & oil pastel

I intended this piece of art to depict God's unfailing protection over Patrick throughout his journey. God asked me to show symbols of His redeeming love and of the darkness He has helped Patrick overcome. The Father looks beyond the actions belying the pain and waits with longsuffering for those whose hearts are towards Him.

Title: *What Is Left Behind* | **Artist:** Victor Franco | 2022; chalk & oil pastel

I intended this piece of art to depict God's continual drawing of Patrick's heart and mind towards Himself. God asked me to show a symbol of the 'treasures of the world'—the things we value on this earth—that He has turned Patrick's attention away from. The Holy Spirit convict and reassures us of our identity and value in Him.

About the Author

Patrick Quezada resides in Colorful Colorado. He is a government employee for the United States Postal Service by day, an active service member/greeter at his local church, a passionate poet, digital creator, influencer, photographer, and an evangelist who has been actively involved in jail ministry. Patrick is the founder of "Taking Back God's Promises" and a member of the "Freedom March Rainbow Revival Movement," which is a community of overcomers who have left behind many labels of sexuality and addiction to follow Jesus Christ.

His mother is grateful to God for Patrick's continued success and restoration. His mother, Rosemarie, shares these words: "To our Heavenly Father be all the glory! I am holding onto the faith, and the promise that God will open up the door for our mother, and son ministry one day. A mother should never have to witness their child being slowly destroyed by the disease called addiction. I am so thankful that we have a God who is able to use all things for His good purpose. The greatest gift I could have ever given my son is passing along the love, and faith that was instilled in me for our God who will never leave us, nor forsake us."

> *"Train up a child in the way he should go: and when he is old, he will not depart from it."* **Proverbs 22:6**

"*A woman giving birth to a child has pain because her time has come; but when her baby is born, she forgets the anguish because of her joy that a child is born into the world.*" **John 16:21**

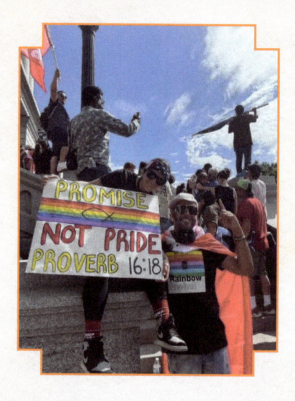

For more information and to connect with me for speaking engagements, prayer requests, and more, please visit my website:

WWW.OPENMYENCRYPTEDHEART.COM

Each request will be handled with the utmost care, confidentiality, and compassion, as I fervently pray for God's guidance, provision, and blessings in your life.

Together, let's walk the path of faith and see how God's grace can revolutionize our lives.

292

Printed in the USA
CPSIA information can be obtained
at www.ICGtesting.com
LVHW070545250924
791926LV00002B/6